Mountain Splendor

BY W. Phillip Keller

Africa's Wild Glory
Canada's Wild Glory
Splendour From the Land
Splendour From the Sea
Under Wilderness Skies
Under Desert Skies
As a Tree Grows
Bold Under God—Charles Bowen
A Shepherd Looks at Psalm 23
A Layman Looks at the Lord's Prayer
Rabboni . . . Which Is to Say, Master
A Shepherd Looks at the Good Shepherd and His Sheep
Taming Tension
Expendable
Mountain Splendor

Mountain Splendor

This is my Father's world

W. Phillip Keller

Fleming H. Revell Company
Old Tappan, New Jersey

Library of Congress Cataloging in Publication Data

Keller, Weldon Phillip, date
    Mountain splendor.

    1. Mountain ecology. 2. Mountains. I. Title.
QH541.5.M65K44   500.9'14'3   78-9778
ISBN 0-8007-0961-6

To
my mountains,

that wondrous, wild realm
which
has ever enriched my life
with inspiring adventures.

Contents

Acknowledgments

A word of thanks first of all to my Heavenly Father for strength of body and freedom of spirit to revel in the high places.

Many thanks to my many mentors, too numerous to mention, who have shared with me their knowledge of the mountains and all wild things.

I am also grateful to my family, who always encouraged and approved of my fierce and loyal love for the high country. In particular, Ursula, who has shown enormous enthusiasm for this book.

Finally, I am indebted to Ernie Owen, field editor of Fleming H. Revell. He quickly caught the burning vision of what such a book could be. But, most important, through his inspiration and advice, he has helped to make another of life's great dreams come to solid reality.

O Lord, how manifold are thy works!
in wisdom hast thou made them all:
the earth is full of thy riches.
                              Psalms 104:24

Preface

The wild, mountain blood of my Swiss forebears flows fiercely in my veins. They were people of the lofty peaks and snowy ranges. Their alpine meadows lying high against the sky, their singing streams, their limpid lakes, their fragrant forests were the fabric of native grandeur woven into their very lives.

Mountain splendor fashioned their culture and molded their strong characters. Theirs was a mountain world that produced a sturdy strain of mountain men—a hardy breed who loved their upthrust land, glorying in her mighty ridges. To survive and flourish in such a challenging environment, they simply had to cherish and husband the rugged resources of their mountain realm.

Forests and fields, streams and lakes, vegetation and wildlife were not theirs to be wasted or squandered through self-indulgence. Rather these were a rich heritage to be conserved with care for posterity, yes, even for their children's children. Their tumbled land was a legacy of love held in trust by each succeeding generation through respect and reverence.

This concept of gentle admiration yet fierce affection for mountains was passed on to me from my parents. My life of adventure in high country has not been restricted to any one region or mountain range. Still, my enduring romance with the ridges has been no less intense than that of those who have spent their entire lives within the shadow of a single mountain system.

Again and again, the world around, mountains have drawn me with a mighty magnetism. Their attraction has been much more than the mere challenge of conquest. It has been the deep desire to move and live amongst them, even if only briefly, in humble awe and wonder. For there is an inspiration, a majesty, to the mountain world that lifts my spirits and stirs my soul to singing.

The mountains are more, much more, than giant heaps of inert rock and rubble. They are more than conglomerations of upthrust fragments of the earth's mantle, often torn and fractured. They are more than mere heights of land, often draped in snow and ice, waiting to be scaled by climbers in search of adventure or skiers in quest of fun.

Mountains are a magnificent realm of ever-changing, ever-shifting patterns of life and light. From their lowest foothills basking in hot summer sun, to their loftiest summits blasted by tremendous blizzards, they are a wonderland of incredible diversity.

Here in this high, tumbled terrain, nothing remains the same. Nothing impresses man as being more permanent than granite peaks; nothing seems more impregnable than the great, glistening ranges of the world. Yet they are ever changing.

The impact of weathering forces, the passing of the seasons, the fluctuations in temperature, the ebb and flow of all the interrelated ecosystems continually modify and alter the mountain environment.

In all of this, up until only very recent times, man's influence has been fairly negligible. Man often has come to the mountains with the sense of a stranger paying a brief visit. If he be humble in mind and receptive in spirit, they speak to him in unmistakable ways.

To some of us, the mountains have given a message of glory and splendor to be shared with our generation. It is not just mighty ridges combing the clouds or glorious ice fields shining in the sun. It is more than rushing rivers surging through wilderness valleys. It far surpasses the sweeping alpine flower fields or the turquoise glacier lakes of the remote places. It is beyond the shy and stately wild creatures of hoof, wing, and claw that make this their home.

In short, *This is my Father's world.* Here He has expressed Himself in unmistakable terms, far more beautiful and breathtaking than mere words can portray.

In part that is why there is included here a selection of photographs which attempt to convey some of that mountain splendor. They are drawn from several thousand slides taken during the hardy, happy years of my mountain rambles.

The mountains have no voice in our council chambers. Yet they can speak emphatically in the sanctuary of our spirits. The forested valleys and flower meadows are silent in the mass media. But their grandeur can be conveyed to those of us who know, understand, and care. The noble wild ones living out their lives in the high ranges are our fellow travelers through space. So a few of us endeavor to speak on their behalf. Perhaps some of their quiet strength can be passed on in peace.

Some of us feel so strongly about this that we cannot remain silent. For a quarter of a century now, I have called aloud for conservation of our natural heritage. From Africa, from Canada, from wilderness areas where still there was time to save a remnant of wilds, my voice has been raised on behalf of my mountain friends. Over and over I have called to my contemporaries to conserve and cherish the irreplaceable heritage given to us by God, our Father.

By books, by magazine articles, by photographs, films, radio broadcasts, television programs, and countless lectures, an attempt has been made to remind my generation that the natural world is not ours to abuse or misuse.

In this book, writing earnestly and honestly as a Christian and a son of the wilds, who cares deeply and profoundly for the earth, I endeavor to remind the reader of our responsibilities under our Father. He has entrusted to our care resources of amazing diversity and wondrous beauty. May we look, listen, learn, and in gentle gratitude act manfully under the inspiration of His generosity.

Thank You, Father, for the mountain splendor of our world!

Mountain Splendor

And God said, Let there be light: and there was light.

Genesis 1:3

1
Mountain Light

A large share of the sheer joy that comes to a man in the mountains is the play of light amongst the peaks. It is light that makes them come alive with ecstatic delight. It may be sunlight, moonlight, or even the dim radiance of starlight. Each provides its own array of moods that quicken the pulse and delight the eye.

I shall never, ever, until the day I can no longer climb a crag, forget my first celestial view of the Rockies. For days I had been traveling slowly westwards across the great, gray prairies gripped by late spring's cold chill. Suddenly, one dawn, I awoke early to see brilliant, brittle sunlight shining and sparkling from the winter snow and blue ice of the Rocky Mountain range on the western horizon.

The sight literally transfixed me. For hundreds of miles north and south, the giant ridges ran along the rim of the earth. The angles of ice and slopes of snow shot back the morning light like rays refracted from a thousand diamond facets. Some of the reflected colors matched the brilliance of a jewel with intense white, blue, and aquamarine hues.

This is the sort of powerful panorama that takes one's breath away. It makes a man, even a tough, hardened man, pause and wonder. Its grandeur can humble our haughty spirits. Its splendor can induce us to walk softly amid its great valleys and ridges.

There is nothing static about light in the high country. It is ever shifting, moving, altering the texture and tone of the landscape. One hour the rock cliffs stand flooded with full, warm light. Their multicolored shades of gray, brown, white, amber, and green lie warmed by sunlight. Yet a few moments later they may stand stark and dark in the shadows. The light will have shifted from their surfaces, leaving them black from lack of light.

On close approach, it is often exciting to discover that it is not just bare, naked rock that is reflecting and transmitting color to our senses. The stern stone faces are sometimes adorned with a score of multi-hued mosses, lichens, and other low-life organisms. Some of these are brilliant greens, chartreuses, golden yellows, rich ochres, silver grays, and brilliant pinks or purples.

Their spores may have been borne a hundred miles on the fickle mountain winds. Finally they found footing on some newly fractured face of rock. There they flourished, to spread themselves audaciously on the surface like comely cosmetics on a lovely woman's countenance. In so doing, they give a particular tone and texture that is that mountain's special adornment.

I recall vividly climbing high in the northern Canadian Rockies one winter. A small band of mountain caribou which had attracted my attention led me over some lofty ridges. Moving stealthily amongst the great, gray outcrops on the summit, I was stalking the handsome bull for close-up photographs. Suddenly I was startled to see a rich display of gray, gold, and orange lichens growing in rich profusion on the fractured stone in front of me. It was a brilliant blue and white winter day. Against this glorious backdrop, the glowing colors of the lowly lichens were beautiful to behold. For a few moments my attention was diverted from the wary caribou herd on the snow slope below me.

With care and immense pleasure I photographed the minute organisms clinging to their precarious perch on this mountain peak. Here in utter solitude, seldom, if ever,

/19

seen by any wandering mountaineer like myself, they lived out their hardy lives in joyous color and vigor. Touched by sunlight, their tiny forms sparkled with ten thousand shining sequins of moisture melted from the snow and sleet that had settled on them in the night.

It was but a momentary interlude in the mountains. Yet it left me with a jewel-bright memory that can never be dimmed or tarnished. There was light, and the light made that intimate moment with lichens live forever—etched indelibly in my mind.

There is this same interplay of light and shadow on snowfields, glaciers, and frozen lakes. It glances and dances from a thousand different directions. Sometimes the reflection is so acute, so intense, it is a blinding brilliance. One must squint and shade the eyes to protect them from its radiance of ultrawhiteness.

This intense illumination lights up the whole mountain world. Shadows of trees, rocks, and animals glow blue, not black. The refracted light bounces everywhere, even filling in the shadows on the snow with subtle tones of delicate turquoise. The landscape is adorned and draped in light that pulses with enormous energy. It lifts our spirits, stimulates our glands, and sets our hearts to quiet singing. It speaks peace. Tranquility settles down softly over our souls.

One September, in an audacious spirit of adventure, I had hiked in alone to a remote and magnificent valley at the foot of the giant Ramparts. The evening I got in, a raging blizzard blew in from the northwest. All night the wind screamed and whined around the ridge pole of the remote mountain cabin. Driven snow grated against the rough log walls.

At dawn all was still. A spotless mantle of immaculate new snow draped the whole world in shining white. As the sun broke over the eastern skyline to flood the landscape in light, my emotions could scarcely be contained. Breathless beauty was everywhere. Majestic splendor surrounded me on every side. Standing there alone—a mere mite of humanity without another man in twenty miles—I was overwhelmed with awe. Majestic mountains towered above me into the brilliant blue sky. The great snow-draped valley swept away in spotless grandeur. And everywhere there was light, light, light.

It was with a deep and moving sense of wonder that I pulled on my big boots, bundled up in my heavy mackinaw, and went out to walk softly in that shining light.

I was not the first to be abroad in the morning sun. I came on a flock of ptarmigan that had sheltered from the storm in a spruce thicket. They were glad to greet the sun. Then I saw a splendid, big bull moose, standing sideways, soaking up the gentle warmth of the golden rays. His hide shone black and brown, his antlers glowed amber in the morning light.

Whatever light touched, it transformed.

It is always thus.

It is part of the endless pageantry of the high country.

Sunlight falling on stone, soil, grass, or leaves gives them shape and substance. The moving shadows cast upon the ground through the overhead canopy of branches, twigs, leaves, cones, and clouds gives the earth a dappled floor covering of ever-changing

colors. Here there is a subtle, shy beauty observed only by those who will take the time to look for it beneath their feet.

Even the bark of trees, the veins on leaves, the fine filigree of intertwined twigs and boughs are sharpened and enhanced by the filtered light falling on them. Sometimes this light is so diffused and delicate that it produces the aura of a sanctuary—a cathedral of quiet repose in the shelter of the trees.

And of course, light on water, be it sunlight or moonlight, has its own peculiar power of multiplying its magic. Be it the surface of a lake, the long run of a river, the tumbling waters of a stream or waterfall, all are mirrors that double the light that falls upon them.

Man has no part in all of this except to perceive it. He can rejoice in its glory. He can give gentle thanks for so great a gift from God, who first brought it into being.

This is ever the sensation which engulfs me as I quietly watch a sunrise or sunset: the sublime silence; the sky reflecting colors which are beautiful in their diversity; the changing, shifting pattern of cloud formations. Yet the whole panorama proceeds without fanfare or proud pronouncements, which would have to be the case if man produced it.

Mornings uncounted I have stood silenced, in quiet awe, watching light steal gently over the eastern ramparts of rock and ice and snow. Slowly the radiance spills over the rim of the earth. It flows into the great basins of the valley bottoms, filling them with sparkling amber sunlight, rich as clear, white wine in a glass goblet.

If the morning skies have been tinged with delicate hues of pink or mauve, these same tints will be reflected from the rugged peaks and slopes first touched with sunlight. Sometimes they glow with red and purple tones so intense that they appear more like an artist's painting than real rock and ice. Slowly, irresistibly, the light moves down the mountainsides. Its warm glow engulfs the landscape in a golden sheen that turns soil and trees, grass and leaves to burnished brass.

These are magic moments in the mountains.

They are fleeting interludes lasting only a few minutes. But they are great enough to stir a man's spirit to its depths.

Greeting the dawn in high country has been a lifetime delight. No two are ever identical. Their variety is unending.

The mountain sunsets can, on occasion, be equally enthralling. There is the quiet hush as the sun slips behind the western ranges. Gently the shadows of the high ridges stretch across the valleys. Light drains from the landscape, and darkness begins to descend beneath the trees.

Softly the line of light steals up the slopes. It changes gradually from white to delicate yellow, then gold, perhaps to rose, then glowing mauve. Briefly the topmost peaks are afire until their flaming colors fade and their last light is quenched like a candle gone out.

Beautiful as light itself can be, it is more, much more than the mere addition of color and tone to the landscape. It is also warmth, cheer, and life itself.

Having carefully observed the life habits of wildlife all my life, their response to light and interaction with its influence are remarkable. The length of daylight hours determines the shifting seasons and patterns of migration. This applies not only to uncounted thousands of birds moving north and south through the mountain world, but also to animals migrating up and down the valleys and slopes in search of fresh forage.

There is also the pure physical pleasure as well as physiological benefit to be derived from simply basking in the sunshine. Insects and birds, small mammals and big game, all revel in the sun. Often their mountain realm is cold, chill, and forbiddingly frigid. So when the warm rays of the sun come streaming in between the ridges, they respond at once to the gentle warmth.

It has often been with a deep and genuine sense of brotherhood that I have found myself sharing a sun-drenched opening in the forest with chipmunks, squirrels, and deer, all of us soaking up sunlight. The chipmunks and squirrels would be sitting out on some extended branch where the warm light made their soft, silky hair shine like spun gold. The deer, elk, or even moose would stand sideways to absorb the full benefit of sunlight shining on their bodies, warming their hides and relaxing their muscles. They just loved it.

A sweet sense of quiet well-being and contentment pervades such interludes. The more so if the night has been cold or wet with rain and sleet and snow. Even in midwinter, wildlife enjoy the feeble warmth that streams from a sun that hangs low above the horizon. It is a gentle sensation of cheer and comfort that tempers the cutting cold and fierce winds that can make the mountains forbidding from fall until spring.

The coming and going of light, the length of day, and the varying temperatures all interact upon the mountain realm to provide eternal change. Under the impulse of temperature fluctuations, rock formations freeze and thaw. Even the most rugged granite will crack and fragment. Frost and ice penetrate the fissures. Their expanding forces shatter the strongest stone. In spring, especially, the high cliffs cannonade with the rumble and roar of giant rockfalls as tons of stone are shoved off the peaks. The tumbling boulders bounce and thunder down the deep draws, loosening other rock and shale in their rush down the steep defiles.

Sometimes these great rockfalls precipitate snowslides, and together stones, snow, ice, and shale roar down the slopes in commingled clouds of dust and snow. Trees and shrubs are torn from their footings and giant gashes are left exposed like new wounds in the mountain's side.

Much the same happens when sunlight warms the slopes, thaws the ice, and loosens snowfields to precipitate avalanches. Thousands of tons of ice and snow hurtle down at tremendous speeds. The snow fans out across the valley floor like a rushing tidal wave, often shearing off trees and shrubs like mere matchsticks. Occasionally a wild mountain sheep or stray deer will be caught in these cascading streams of snow and ice. The next summer their carcasses will be seen strewn amongst the shale and debris left behind when the snow and ice have melted away.

In contrast to all this violent demolition in the mountain terrain, light goes on gently doing its profound upbuilding by means of photosynthesis. Falling upon mosses and lichens, grasses and plants, shrubs and trees, the manufacture of new life is stimulated by light and warmth. Perennials burst anew from the barren winter landscape. Snow lilies, mountain anemones, and a thousand other wild flowers and plants flourish in the few short weeks of the mountain summer. Grass and shrubs and trees put on new growth, covering the slopes in tender greens. All of this our Father has arranged and planned with magnificent precision and purpose. Man has had no part in the program.

*And God said, Let there be a firmament
in the midst of the waters, and let it di-
vide the waters from the waters.*

Genesis 1:6

2
Mountain Waters

Water, like fire, is one of the major agencies that gives mountains their unique character. Water in various forms has been at work upon the planet, shaping and sculpting its surface since the dawn of time. The very fact that moisture and water in free form exist in the earth's atmosphere accounts for the unique and wondrous topography of this terrestrial ball.

Some of the world's great mountain ranges are composed of sedimentary rocks laid down initially as silt and marine deposits beneath the seas. Giant upheavals of the earth's mantle in subsequent eras thrust the fragmented seabed upwards. Fractured and broken by the dislocation, great blocks of sedimentary stone stood on edge to form giant ranges. Even on the summits of some of their highest peaks, we can recover preserved specimens of marine life that once lay on the bottom of the ocean floor.

Over the great eons of time since its initial formation, gigantic floods and raging, great rivers have coursed back and forth over the earth. Alternating periods of ice and moderate temperatures have moved masses of ice and snow (frozen water) back and forth across the globe like enormous scrapers and chisels. They planed and gouged out the grim visages of the earth's main features in temperate latitudes. And this work still goes on. Glaciers advance and recede, cutting out valleys, throwing up moraines, and all the time grinding down stone to glacial flour finer than any man-made mill could manufacture.

So when a man goes to hike in the high country, he is instantly made aware that he is in a realm where water is at work in a multitude of ways.

35

The high peaks and lofty ranges comb the clouds and divert the moisture-laden winds that encircle the globe. The rising air, forced upward across the windward faces of the rock formations, is freed of its moisture that drops earthward in the form of snow and rain and mist.

The cloud-shrouded slopes drip with wetness. Sometimes for weeks at a time sunlight scarcely reaches through the enfolding canopy of fog, mist, clouds, and snowstorms that wrap themselves about the windward shoulders of the hills. There is a steady, almost unrelenting deposition of snow, sleet, rain, or mist upon the mountain slopes.

On the leeward side, this phenomenon is less pronounced. In the rain shadow of the ranges, rain and snow are much more intermittent. The sun breaks through the cloud cover at frequent intervals, and the terrain is warmed with mellow sunlight.

This variation in the amount of water that is precipitated on the peaks and ranges in any given season produces an amazing diversity of vegetation. One side of a mountain may be smothered under the rank growth of a rain forest that drips moisture like a giant sponge spread over hundreds of square miles. On the opposite face there may be open, sparse grasslands, alpine flower fields, and, in some rare cases, almost desertlike conditions where only the most hardy, drought-resistant plants can survive the arid climate.

All of this lends enormous diversity and interest to the mountain world. Not only does it provide a great array of plant life, but also of animal life adapted to the various types of flora. And naturally there is likewise an in redible variety of scenery, depending upon the vegetative cover which adorns the terrain.

Amid all these various mountain landscapes, water is ever present both in sight and sound. It is inescapable. There are the overhanging clouds of rain and snow and mist that swirl like white and gray shawls around the shoulders of the hills. There is the song and sparkle of springs gurgling from beneath the ground. There is the tumbling, happy laughter of streams leaping and bounding down the slopes. There is the sullen roar of the rivers growling over the boulders in their beds, rushing with white water over the rapids, thundering through the narrow canyons and gorges that would restrict their flow. There is the white mist and floating spray that rise from the waterfalls. Great streams of falling, frothing water that leap and bound across the ledges of rock, to be lost in white foam. There are the still pools and quiet lakes; the marshes, ponds, and swamps; the gentle places where water rests and casts its mellow mood upon the harried soul of man.

All of this has been beautifully portrayed in picture language by the psalmist who wrote centuries ago:

Thou coveredst it with the deep as with a garment: the waters stood above the mountains. At thy rebuke they fled; at the voice of thy thunder they hasted away. They go up by the mountains; they go down by the valleys unto the place which thou hast founded for them. Thou hast set a bound that they may not pass over; that they turn not again to cover the earth. He sendeth the springs into the valleys, which run among the hills. They give drink to every beast of the field: the wild asses quench their thirst. By them shall the fowls of the heaven have their habitation, which sing among the branches. He watereth the hills from his chambers: the earth is satisfied with the fruit of thy works.

Psalms 104:6–13

Even in the grimmest mountain setting, it is remarkable how the presence of moisture, interacting with light, can suddenly transform an austere scene into a panorama of exquisite beauty.

I recall two such incidents which occurred on the same beloved Crater Mountain, some ten years apart. One spring a friend and myself had forced our way up, through old, decaying drifts of winter snow, to the summit. A belated March storm was sending its last, struggling remnants of sleet and hail over the rock bluffs. Its flying ice particles stung our faces while the wind-driven clouds shrouded the slopes in deep, dark folds. One could not see more than a few short yards through the gloom and overcast. Trees and rocks and slopes were vague, dark shapes that came and went silently in the dim light. It seemed pointless to spend more time on the mountain, when I sensed a sudden lifting of the overcast.

In a matter of minutes the trailing veils of snow clouds and gray sleet shrouds began to dissipate. Strongly, the light from the late afternoon sun intensified. Then, with a burst of splendor, it flooded the slopes with golden radiance. To my unbounded delight, the whole summit stood starkly beautiful, sprinkled with a light dusting of new snow. Every stone, blade of grass, and tree twig glistened with wetness. And over it all there arched one of the most radiant, pulsing rainbows, framing the scene with rich color.

As if this in itself were not enough, suddenly there was a startled movement on the rock bluffs above us. A wild band of sixteen bighorn mountain sheep raced up the slope and stood like statues cast in bronze in the golden sunlight. Over them arched the spectacular bow, completing a sight that will never be erased from the rich, full pages of my memory.

This was a momentary, fleeting, passing spectacle witnessed by two men on a mountain. But its joyous impact and heart-thumping thrill endure forever.

Just last autumn another friend and myself had been up on this same mountain all day. It is a favorite area for us. It lies only about an hour's drive from our homes, yet embraces wild, untamed terrain that we both love. Again it had been a dull, wet, stormy day on the slopes. Apart from a few grouse on the trail, there had been little wildlife to enliven the day's tramp.

As evening approached we descended the slopes and were working our way gently down the valley of the Ashnola River. As if to bid us farewell, the late sun broke through the clouds, pouring its golden light into the steep-sided canyons. The poplars, wet with moisture, glistened like gold in their multi-hued tones of yellow, orange, and bronze. The great trees arched over the stream like cathedral arches adorned with gold leaf. Beneath their branches, the stream tumbled over its rocks in spangled, splashing, rapids of commingled blue and white water. It was an utterly breathtaking setting, combining water, light, trees, rocks, and shrubs in a moving scene.

Once more, we suddenly saw a movement on the riverbank that caught our eyes. Two powerful bighorn rams, strong in the rut, were doing battle beneath the trees. It was as if they were special actors on center stage, surrounded with a gorgeous backdrop of golden foliage and blue white waters that doubly enhanced the grandeur of their own strong, muscled bodies.

Moments like these make an indelible imprint on the mind. There is nothing artificial or contrived about them. They are not in any sense "staged." They spring spontaneously from the basic elements of beauty which are an inherent part of the mountain world. When they do come upon a man or woman who is sensitive in spirit, it is with the intense, overwhelming awareness that we are in the presence of divine artistry. This is the sort of thing which only God, our Father, in His amazing resourcefulness, could arrange. Sometimes a few of us earth men are there to witness the pageantry and bow our hearts in humble gratitude. More often, much more often, the quiet, joyous scenes come and go, enacted without any audience except the native wildlife of the region.

It has been my great good fortune, during a life of wilderness wanderings, to witness hundreds and hundreds of beautiful interludes in the high country. Many of these it has been possible to record on film. Some have never been so preserved, simply because the

camera was not slung over my shoulder. Yet in no way are they less precious, because our memories have the incredible capacity to record and store them in the vaults of our remembrance. There they are bullion which no one can ever steal or take from us. And when the day comes that legs and lungs are no longer able to bear us to the heights, we can still sit beside a crackling fire and draw rich memories from our memory files to be relived uncounted times.

It is not only the interplay of light and moisture, shadows and brightness, which our memories can replay. There are also the subtle, pungent aromas produced by rain and dew and mist.

The fragrance of the forest floor after rain is something very special to one who loves the feel of pine needles and fallen leaves beneath his feet. A delicate aroma of decaying leaf mold reminds the passerby that the ancient processes of organic decomposition go on steadily. By the interaction of warmth, moisture, and bacterial activity, leaves, twigs, bark, cones, and dead animal matter are converted to rich, friable soil that will support new plant life.

The sweetness of the air after a passing shower is akin to the most delicate perfume. Depending on the terrain, it may bear the assorted aromas of pine, spruce, fir, larch, aspen, sagebrush, rabbit bush, anemones, wild roses, or even spring violets. These fragrances are wafted here and there on the mountain breezes. They titillate our nostrils, heighten the awareness of our world, and sharpen the accent of the season.

One of my favorite delights is to walk softly through a grove of poplars, in the spring, after an April shower. As the buds of the balm of Gilead swell and burst beneath the influences of sun and moisture, the sweet, sugary sap rising in the trees spreads its exquisite fragrance on the air. It is a heady aroma. It stirs the blood, quickens the pulse, and stimulates the senses with the acute awareness—*spring is here.*

Another great benefit of moisture in the mountains is the softness and stillness it brings. A man can move through the woods and across the meadows in almost total silence. There is, underfoot, a cushion of soft resilience. Twigs and leaves and grass and cones do not crackle and snap like tissue paper as they do when they're dry. It is an aid to the person who comes to tread quietly, linger long, and revel in the company of his other wild companions of hoof, wing, or claw.

And, of course, rain, dew, mist, fog, and snow are the great eternal deterrents that restrain the raging forest fires which are ever a part of the mountain scene.

It is in the high country that the music of water in motion produces a thousand melodies. Sometimes it is the barely audible tinkle of crystal drops within the blue and white dome of a glacier's ice cave. It may be the gentle gurgle of clear, cool liquid gently springing from the ground beneath green banks of moss. Often it is the soft, still swirl of smooth streams surging amid the grass flats and willow thickets of the upland meadows where intricate oxbows are shaped in the sod. There in the alplands, depending on the shifting mountain air, there is the rise and fall of the sounds of falling water. Like the music of a great orchestra in a giant amphitheater, the music of falling water tumbling over the rock faces is amplified or diminished beneath the baton of the breezes.

48/

Further down, in the giant valleys and gorges, stream meets stream and water joins water in rushing white foam. It surges through the narrows, thundering over its rocky bed; it leaps wildly over ridges of stone, with frothing whiteness; then plunges majestically in billowing clouds over precipices where its roar reverberates with mighty echoes across the cliffs. It is the music of power, the melody of water returning to the sea from whence it came, borne upon the mountain winds.

Often I have stood alone on a stream bank or river verge and listened long to its glorious song. If it is glacier-fed, the music will be muted in the morning, for then the mountain realm is chill and still. But beneath the heat of the day, with summer sun accelerating runoff, the melody will change. Gradually the rising flow will grow in grandeur, mounting to a majestic crescendo as the powerful water adds to its own sound the rumble of rolling rock within its current, which reminds the listener of the clash of mighty cymbals and dull thunder of distant drums.

At such moments a man stands humbly awed by his Father's world. It is a world not only for him to harness for hydroelectric energy, but also a world in which his soul may find both joyous refreshment and cause to worship quietly.

3
Mountain Land Forms

Mountains are mountains by virtue of the fact that the earth's crust has been wrinkled by titanic forces at work within the planet. Some of these forces are volcanic in origin. Others have been induced by the tremendous movement of continental plates pressing against each other. Whatever the initial cause, the thin skin of the planet has been strained, buckled, and shoved up into mountain ranges, foothills, and rugged valleys.

This crinkling of the land surface has given to each area its own peculiar texture and form. Some mountains, just newly formed, are gauntly beautiful in their rugged, raw grandeur. Others, ancient with millennia of weathering, have been worn away into unique terrain of winsome delight.

The constant gnawing and grating of wind and water, ice and snow, rain and runoff shape and sculpt the earth into myriad land forms of amazing diversity. And it is this variation in topography which provides so much interest for the mountain enthusiast.

The Canadian Rockies, a very ancient range worn down like a set of very old teeth, have a quality about them totally distinct from the much younger Selkirk Range just a few miles to the west.

The Rockies, exposed to countless millennia of glaciation, have a squared-off, blocky, sturdy appearance. By contrast, the peaks of the Selkirks are sharp, steep, jagged daggers, not yet weathered down to the stumplike form of their eastern companions.

Likewise, depending on the actual rock to be found in any given area, the colors and tints of mountains vary enormously. Some are gray with granite. Others may be almost black with basalt. In the southwest desert regions of the United States there are purple, red, orange, and yellow mountains of exquisite beauty.

In any given mountain system there will be an amazing diversity of strata in the stone. Under the molding, heaving, upthrust pressures that produced them, layers of rock sometimes stand out in startling bands of gray, brown, black, white, and red rock. Like the icing on a cake, they may be twisted and curled into amazing contortions. The forces capable of such colossal convulsions overwhelm our imaginations because they are beyond our human experience.

Often, while climbing in the high country, I have stood awestruck, in humble amazement, gazing at whole ranges that looked like the curling, swirling waves of the sea set in stone. Nor were these just small hills of a few hundred feet height. Rather they are gigantic ranges thrust up thousands of feet from the valley floor.

Sometimes these faces of rock, heaved up toward the heavens by titanic internal forces within the earth itself, are the open book which a geologist can read with ease. Especially so if the terrain has been bared to sun and wind and rain. There is no overburden of debris or accumulated vegetation to hide the native material from which the mountain emerged. There is something very basic, very stern, very strong in intimate contact with such landscapes.

Though poets, writers, and philosophers throughout human history have repeatedly resorted to mountains as the final earth form of durability, it is not an essentially valid concept. It is true that when measured against the brief span of a man's life, they are of long duration. It is likewise true that when compared with the constantly changing

patterns of other planetary life forms, mountains do have a majestic atmosphere of durability about them. Still the basic fact remains that they are not eternal.

Our Heavenly Father, God, who first conceived of the universe, who by special plan and with intelligent activity created the galaxies, is alone eternal. And though numberless stars, suns, moons, and lesser satellites populate space, none of them are eternal. All are either in a condition of creation or decay.

This important principle applies to any mountain a man may set his boot upon. And even though the rock ramparts over which he climbs like a minute ant struggling over a stone appear to him ever enduring in their formidable grandeur, it simply is not so. Any mountain anywhere upon the globe, be it in the Antarctic or at the equator, is being ground down, worn away by the irresistible weathering of planetary forces.

No one knows precisely where stands the most ancient or loftiest mountain range. Some whose bases are thousands of feet below the ocean surface may very well exceed the Himalayas. Not all of the earth's submarine mountains have yet been fully charted or measured in mass. For example, the gentle, rolling dome of Mauna Loa, in Hawaii, far exceeds in actual height, from base to crest, that of Mount Everest in the Himalayas. And as the earth's crust continues to convulse, we may well expect new land forms to emerge from beneath the sea or burst in violence from some fault line upon the planet where the surface is fractured.

With all of this as a background, a man goes to the mountains with a humble heart and quiet mind. For despite the constant changes in their characters, they still speak to us of solidity and endurance. Amid a world of accelerating changes, they lend to us a sense of longevity which we respect and enjoy. For seldom in a single man's lifetime do mountains change enough to be noticeable. Most of the time they appear so very solid and unchangeable that we actually derive repose and reassurance from being in their happy company.

Yet in this realm, as in every other area of life, there can be sudden and drastic changes in the contours of the landscape. Two classic illustrations are the Hope Slide in British Columbia and the Frank Slide in Alberta. Both of these titanic rockfalls that thundered down the mountain slopes wiped out human life and buried homes and roads under millions of tons of stone. In a matter of minutes the entire mountain configuration was altered beyond recognition. The same can happen with volcanoes, avalanches, and enormous mud slides.

Beyond all of this, mountain landscapes, for most of us, are symbolic of solidity and strength. They speak in muted tones of that which lasts. And really, it is this mood of might and majesty which contributes so richly to our moments amid the peaks.

We see storms swirl and surge around the rugged crest of a proud monarch. Sleet, hail, rain, and snow are hurled in fury at the summit. But when the worst is over and the sun shines again, the mountain stands more regal than before. It may even be enhanced with a fresh dusting of new snow or sparkle shining clean, washed by rain. Essentially the mountain itself does not seem to have changed, except very superficially, and that in a rather cosmetic way.

So there is combined both an enduring quality of what seems to us a never-changing inner solidarity, overlaid by an exciting ever-changing external ornamentation. If we spend much time in mountain country, this in fact becomes one of the chief stimulations to our souls. The same range in winter looks totally different from the way it looks in summer. The same ridges under storm clouds are a far cry from what they look like under open skies and golden sunlight. The mountain landscapes appear to actually change form, not only from season to season and weather to weather, but also from hour to hour. Shadows shift and topography fades or intensifies depending upon the light falling upon angles of rock, slopes of scree, glacial faces, or fields of snow.

In all of this there is enormous excitement. There is nothing static about mountain scenes. Any mountain painter will confirm how quickly the color must be applied to the canvas to capture the mood of the moment. There is constant motion, change, and altered accent of rock formations. There is the shift of color, the subtle gradation of tones that take us by surprise. All of it enriches our interludes in the mountain ranges. From dawn, when their regal crowns glow like gold, to dusk, when the last pale pink fades off the stern stone faces, the mighty monarchs overwhelm us with their mountain splendor.

It is only when a man or woman actually sets foot upon a mountain that his or her sense of proportion is brought into proper perspective. It is not enough to fly over it in an aircraft, to drive through it in a car or bus, or even scramble over its rough trails on motorbikes or horseback. One simply has to accept its challenge with bone and blood and bare flesh to discover how truly immense and inspiring this gigantic mound of rock can be to the human heart.

It is against the personal, private measurement of a climber's strength of body and receptivity of soul that mountains are properly appraised. They are not there just to challenge a climber's skill in ascending some difficult rock face. Nor is their true majesty made known only to the hardy hiker who can proudly plant his nailed boot on the

highest cornice of snow or summit of a stony spire. Rather they are there as a symbol of quiet strength, to be shared with anyone who will come to spend time humbly amongst their peaks and valleys.

This means a man must be open in spirit. He must be ready to listen. For the mountains can and will speak peace to him who is attuned to their voices. They can overwhelm him with contentment and wonderment. They can send him away much richer in memory than when he came. In essence that is what this book, its photographs, its reflections, its theme, is all about.

Again and again I have gone to the mountains, mountains all over the world, great mountains as magnificent as the Hindu Kush Range in West Pakistan or Kilimanjaro in East Africa, and little mountains no larger than the Cathedrals or Gold Range in back of my home, yet always I return refreshed.

The giant ridges of rock, the enormous cliffs that dwarf a man, the shining snowfields reflecting the sun, the deep gorges where white water thunders in the canyons, the undulating foothills draped in forests or grass slopes, the upthrust peaks combing the clouds, the sweeping valleys with their singing streams all speak peace, all breathe hope.

But beyond this, they gently call me to come and spend some precious moments in their company. This is no man-made world. This is no realm where the will of man is paramount. Instead it is a region where I come as a guest to share the bounty and riches which are provided by my Father.

and shadow, the wide vistas over valleys and plains and ridges: Man could take no credit for any of this. It was not of his making or manipulation. His pride and intellectual genius had no part in it. These land forms in all their magnificence had stamped upon them MADE BY GOD.

Here we see in rich and lavish display a thousand vistas which, from the dawn of human history, have stirred and inspired artists, writers, poets, musicians, and ordinary men. Much that is fine, noble, and lofty in any human culture was and has been cradled in the unspoiled wilderness. It is the crucible from which has come the finest of literature, art, music, and ornamentation. These were initiated, not in the mind of man, but in the mind of God, our Father, who first conceived them.

Everywhere we turn in the mountains, we discover order, symmetry, and design of breathtaking proportions. The intricate patterns eroded in earth and rock by running water are precisely duplicated ten million upon ten million times in the vein patterns of tree leaves. Descend to the seashore and see identical designs etched in sand when the tide recedes.

Examine the strata of rock and stone laid down layer upon layer in the vast millennia of mountain building: a process of long and painstaking deliberation either by the deposition of debris upon the ocean floor or the overlay of volcanic action across millennia of time. The same principle is at work in the trunk of a tree, where cell is added to cell, layer upon layer of wood is multiplied from season to season to form concentric rings of gorgeous grain, wondrous in beauty.

If we come with open minds and humble spirits, we discern a profound pageantry played out upon the planet. None of it has happened either by accident or chance. Long, long before ever man set foot upon the stage, this had been programmed in the council chambers of eternity. All the ongoing earth systems which have brought to this particular planet such beauty, music, and life had their origin in my Father's mind. It is He who supervises their performance. It is He who initially thought of them. It is He who set them in motion. It is He who sees their ultimate end. And it is He who maintains them with meticulous momentum.

All of this sweeps over my soul when I move amongst the mountains. And in such awareness I join the ancient psalmist in irrepressible praise.

The heavens declare the glory of God; and the firmament sheweth his handywork. Day unto day uttereth speech, and night unto night sheweth knowledge. There is no speech nor language, where their voice is not heard. Their line is gone out through all the earth, and their words to the end of the world. In them hath he set a tabernacle for the sun, Which is as a bridegroom coming out of his chamber, and rejoiceth as a strong man to run a race. His going forth is from the end of the heaven, and his circuit unto the ends of it: and there is nothing hid from the heat thereof. The law of the Lord is perfect, converting the soul: the testimony of the Lord is sure, making wise the simple.

Psalms 19:1–7

And God said, Let the earth bring forth grass, the herb yielding seed, and the fruit tree yielding fruit after his kind, whose seed is in itself, upon the earth: and it was so.

Genesis 1:11

4
Mountain Meadows and Forests

Mountains are much more than just great, upthrust masses of rock and soil. They are more than gigantic ridges and pinnacles of stone sheathed in ice and snow. They are more than lofty peaks that puncture the sky, drawing veils of mist and cloud about their regal shoulders.

They are also enormous sanctuaries for multitudinous life forms. Their diversity and array of vegetation is almost infinite in its display. Depending upon the latitude and elevation of the terrain, plant life present can vary from colossal forest giants to the most minute grasses and herbs clinging precariously to some tiny ledge of stone.

No man moving through this landscape can help but be enormously impressed by the variety of trees and shrubs, mosses and lichens, grasses and flowers which adorn the high country. For example, the western mountain region of North America alone produces roughly four thousand different wild flowers. Some of these are flung across the alplands in fantastic fields of glorious color. Others are to be found blooming very shyly in secluded spots where only diligent searching will disclose their hiding places.

Much the same is true of trees. Some slopes are almost solid stands of a single species. I have found forests of lodgepole pine, like the humble jack pine, that covered mile upon mile of mountain country. Scarcely another kind of tree was to be found, except perhaps an occasional Douglas fir that had managed to survive the raging forest fires which gave rise to the lowly pines.

On the other hand, some mountain forests are composed of many different species. These flourish together in rich and luxurious profusion. It is not uncommon to find firs, pines, cedars, hemlocks, and other lesser trees growing together in happy communities.

The great mountain forests that clothe the foothills and lower flanks of mountains are in themselves wondrous worlds. Here the mountain winds and storms are stilled. The winter gales and blustering blizzards are hushed. The summer heat is tempered. Here a man treads softly, his feet cushioned by the carpet of accumulated leaves, twigs, needles, and bark that have fallen from ten million trees.

In these shadowed isles, the shy creatures of hoof, wing, and paw move softly. Like actors on a silent stage, they slip through the softly dappled light that streams down through the green canopy of branches. Only now and then is the enfolding silence of the great trees broken by some sudden sound. Perhaps the shrill staccato chatter of a squirrel, the snort of a startled deer, the raucous cry of a raven, or the sudden "snap" of a dead twig breaking off a branch stabs the cloistered stillness.

The intense quiet of a mighty forest is a most formidable and forbidding environment for those not accustomed to its deep serenity. One can almost sense the surge of his own small lifestream pulsing through his blood vessels. The steady, even pumping of his own heart is a rhythm in harmony with the powerful impulse of life all around him, all one in the earth's great, interwoven web of life.

Here the clamorous, clanging cacophony of man's world is hushed. Here the soul and spirit are still in the presence of pristine solitude. Here a man can sense and know something of his own insignificance.

The gigantic trunks of Douglas firs, redwoods, western cedars, and Sequoias dwarf his own tiny frame. They sweep up to the clouds in massive columns of majestic strength, lifting their life-giving sap hundreds of feet against the eternal drag of gravity. Thrust against the sky, their strong limbs and proud crowns have bravely faced ten thousand winter storms and as many summer suns.

There is something deeply moving about these great forests that calls to us. They are amongst the oldest and most enduring life forms upon the planet. Their ancient lineage is exceeded only by the tough and hardy bristlecone pines of the Southwest deserts.

As a man strolls in the shadow of their forest aisles, as he lays his little hand upon their giant buttresses, as he allows his eyes to travel up their tall trunks, his pride is pressed down within him. His jaunty arrogance is subdued momentarily. His inner spirit responds to the grandeur about him and cries out, *Only God could make a tree. . . .*

Not just *one* tree, but ten million upon ten million other trees. Each is a marvel of majestic design and exquisite intricacy. Each tree has found its foothold upon the earth in a site suited to its survival. There it spreads its green glory beneath the sun. There it stands strong and steady for fifty, a hundred, maybe even a thousand years, enduring winter storms and summer sun. It shades the earth, tempers the air, binds the soil, and sings in the breezes that blow about its boughs.

For me a forest is a wonderland of variety. When I walk in any wooded area, it is ever

with a sense of awe and reverence lying gently upon me. The forest floor itself is alive with deep-piled mosses. Gorgeous ferns grace the moist places. They flourish along streams and revel in the sparkling spray of waterfalls. Shade-loving shrubs and plants proliferate in the understory of the trees. There they bloom shyly and bear their fruit in quiet seclusion.

From time immemorial huge forest fires have engulfed the forests. The roaring flames rush through the trees, generating an inferno of heat which no living thing can endure. The fire itself often creates its own tremendous updraft. This sends the flames leaping from tree to tree in a bursting, blinding rush that can blacken a mountain in minutes.

When the fire has passed, only desolation seems to linger in its wake. The skeletons of the trees stand bleak and black against the sky. Ash and charcoal cover the slopes, which are stripped bare. To the unknowing eye, all appears dead. And briefly this is so, but not for too long.

The heat of the passing flames has burst open the cones of fire-resistant trees. Soon there sprouts from the charred ground a new green growth of seedlings. Borne on the mountain winds, too, come a sprinkling of feathery seeds produced by pioneer plants. Fireweed, dandelions, thistles, willow, and a dozen different, hardy, tough plants seed themselves in the giant burns. A whole new complex of vegetation invades the open spaces.

Season after season the fire-killed forest turns gradually from black to gray to silver. The skeletons of the once-green trees take on a shining silver sheen that sparkles in the sun. It becomes a "silver forest," rich with pioneer plants that support an abundance of wildlife.

Here is where the lush green herbs, new grasses, berry patches, and low browse abound. Wide open to sunlight, enriched by the minerals in the ashes, plants that take root in fire burns are high in nutrition. So it is to these places wildlife come to gorge themselves. Moose, elk, deer, ground squirrels, chipmunks, bears, birds, and scores of other life forms find the old burns a happy feeding ground.

All of this is a pageantry played out upon the mountains without man's manipulation. It is an ancient drama enacted all over the high country. Forests come, forests go. One plant community succeeds another. Some trees survive to become venerated veterans. Others are swept away in fires, avalanches, storms, or floods. Yet amid all the changing scenes, life continues unabated, undiminished. It is part and parcel of our Father's remarkable provision for the enrichment of the planet. New and diverse species of trees, shrubs, plants, and grasses proliferate wherever natural forces create a fresh habitat suited to their survival.

The intense excitement and deep delight of watching all of this take place are part of the joy in mountain interludes. I have hiked across mountain meadows and alpine flower fields which in very truth took my breath away with their beauty. To see thousands of acres of upland slopes spangled with drifts of wild flowers, not one of which was planted by a man's hand, is a moving experience. It is a solemn reminder of the initial reaction God had when He looked upon His original creation "and saw that it was good."

There are few experiences available to us that can equal the privilege of spending a few weeks in high country above timberline in midsummer. For sheer beauty of setting and variety of landscape, there is nothing that quite matches the majesty of alpine mountain meadows. When I say this, I am bearing in mind the stark beauty of multicolored deserts, the wide sweep of great plains and open veld, the splendor of picturesque seascapes, and the loveliness of rural landscapes. Exquisite as any of these may be, it is still true to say that the high country above tree line under summer skies is a realm removed from and transcending all others in inspiration.

Often, in this mountain terrain, Psalms 104:16–18 is brought to my remembrance.

> The trees of the Lord are full of sap; the cedars of Lebanon, which he hath planted; Where the birds make their nests: as for the stork, the fir trees are her house. The high hills are a refuge for the wild goats; and the rocks for the conies.

This impression steals over one's spirit very noticeably as the trail through the forest gains altitude. Gradually the giants of the fertile valley bottoms and lower slopes give way to more modest timber. There is a pronounced reduction in the size and scale of the

trees. The species replace each other. At the higher levels, their limbs are shorter, stiffer, sometimes downward sloping, the better to bear the heavy loads of snow and sleet dumped upon them by wild winter storms.

Here and there, great breaks of skyline show through the thinning stands of timber. There will be a glimpse of a gleaming peak or a shining snowfield soaring above the trees. A quickening pulse and pounding heartbeat reflect not only the increasing altitude, but also the mounting excitement of new vistas.

The mountain air becomes more pungent with the sweet, delicious aroma of spruce and pine and fir. It is a heady, stimulating fragrance, borne on the breezes that drift down from the cool snowfields. It titillates one's nostrils. There is the immediate impulse to inhale deeply, expanding the lungs, letting the clear, crisp air rush with vigor through veins and arteries.

Suddenly the trail breaks out of the trees. It is almost like magic. Although I have climbed scores and scores of mountains, the surprising suddenness with which a man moves from forest into flower fields has always thrilled and surprised me. All at once, it seems, the trees end and the open meadows commence.

Of course, depending on the terrain, the fringe between the two areas can vary in beauty. Sometimes it resembles a manicured park with individual trees of perfect shape scattered across the landscape either singly or in clusters. In other places the meadows have dwarfed, weather-beaten trees that look like misshapen shrubs.

Undulating up the slopes, lie gorgeous green meadows. Like great rugs spangled with splashes of red, white, mauve, pink, yellow, and blue, they drape the alplands in a cascade of color. In wild abandon and gay profusion, hordes of lupines, Indian paintbrush, anemones, lilies, buttercups, and a hundred other flowers spread themselves beneath the sun, blowing in the breeze.

This in itself would be enough to overwhelm us with joy. But set all this beauty amid giant amphitheaters of mountain ridges, shining snowfields, alpine lakes, silver streams, and glistening glaciers; at times it is almost too much to take in. We wonder, *Can it be true? Is it real? Or is this the garden of the gods?*

It may well be that the alpine meadows could be called the garden of the gods, but for me, as a Christian, they are the garden of God: my Father's flower fields. They are of His creation, arranged and ordered by His inspiration. Not one of the billions of bulbs, seeds, or shoots needed to establish these magnificent gardens came from a man's hand, nor was one set in place by human labor.

Year after year, season upon season, the wild glory of this alpine country perpetuates itself. And this is no little thing, for at these high altitudes the climate and habitat are formidable and fierce. Some mountain meadows are free of frost only six weeks in the year. During that brief interlude, a plant must spring from the chill soil, make its full annual growth, flower in full bloom, then set seed to reproduce the species. A truly remarkable performance!

Some of the plants are rooted in such sparse and stony soil and at such lofty levels that their size is dwarfed to minute proportions. Whole plants are sometimes no larger in diameter than a small pocketknife. Yet each is complete and entire in its perfection.

What has been said about the grandeur of the sweeping fields of wild flowers applies equally to the "rock gardens" that grow amid the high ridges and outcrops of rocks. The unique arrangements of wind-stunted trees, hardy shrubs, and tough flowering plants that anchor themselves amongst the weathered stone are remarkable to behold.

Again and again in some small nook or corner, sheltered from the stormy blast of wind and blizzards, I have found fantastic plant communities. In fact the initial inspiration that has led to the whole world of rockeries originated here in the high country. Often only the toughest of plant life can survive the fierce onslaught of terrifying winter weather most of the year.

It is not uncommon in the mountain meadows to find twisted, tortured little trees hundreds of years old that have grown only a few feet tall. Some of them will have stout, sturdy trunks as thick as a man's thigh, yet their full height may not exceed three or four feet. For perhaps eight months of the year they will be buried beneath snow or sheathed in ice and sleet. Their shapes are determined by the prevailing winds which whip and lash their branches mercilessly, driving them to grow in only one direction. Some, to survive, can only spread themselves along the ground in lowly, prostrate shapes.

Yet each of these, in its own intimate way, is a thing of beauty. They convey a character of fortitude, endurance, and strength that has been produced by uncounted storms that raged across the heights. It is always with a sense of quiet awe and deep admiration that I move amongst these alpine trees or shelter beneath their boughs. Of these I have written at length in my book *As a Tree Grows.*

Any man or woman who has spent some weeks or months in this high country is richer for it. A new and enlarged dimension has been added to life. An awareness that indeed this is a majestic segment of his Father's world, settles down upon the soul in quiet peace.

5
Mountain Seasons

Seasons in the high country are quite unlike the same seasons in the lowlands. The most obvious reason for this is, of course, the difference in altitude. There on the highest peaks, almost eternal winter, with storms of sleet and ice and snow, prevails. But this is true of only the very loftiest levels. For most mountain terrain in temperate regions there is a definite rhythm of spring and summer, autumn and winter.

In thinking of these, one has to be very realistic and understand that winter can come very early and linger very late. Spring can be but a stormy interlude before summer settles in softly for a few short weeks. Finally fall, the time of great glory under Indian summer skies, ends in all too brief interludes of still days with their glowing colors.

Only those who have spent much time in the mountains learn to hold their wild weather in profound respect. It is the passing parade of eternal seasons that determines, to a large degree, what varieties of trees, shrubs, plants, and lower life forms shall survive. It is the severity of the seasons also which decides what species of animals, birds, and insects will find a habitat here to guarantee their survival.

All of the interlocking facets of climate, altitude, precipitation of rain or snow, temperatures, soil, moisture, and latitude are a finely woven web. Within its interlaced pattern, a great array of plant and animal life is continually endeavoring to adapt itself to the ever-changing habitat. Here there is a continuous state of flux. Amid the ebb and flow of the seasons, life continues.

This stream of life takes many forms. It may be the lowliest and most simple lichens, whose spores have been blown onto a fresh face of fractured stone shattered by the forces of frost. There they flourish, flinging their fragile beauty across the rock. Yet, to endure and survive they must be terribly tough, terribly tenacious in spite of raging winds, driving sleet, and the abrasive action of a thousand storms.

The stream of life may be moving in a prolific insect community. Mosquitoes, for example, that in some mountain valleys swarm in uncounted billions during the summer, suddenly disappear with the sharp, killing frosts of fall. Their eggs have been laid and through the long winter remain refrigerated in the deep freeze of heavy snow. Yet, the following June, with the warm touch of summer sun, they emerge to swarm across the sun-dappled meadows and marshes.

The ongoing stream of bird life perpetuates itself in various ways. Some escape the atrocious winter weather by moving out of the mountains altogether. They fly great distances to warmer latitudes. Some cross thousands of miles of uncharted terrain to finally set foot in some more salubrious surroundings. Yet hardy species such as grouse, ptarmigan, and ravens will tough it out through the year. They may move short distances down the mountain slopes into the shelter of timber and brush, where sufficient feed and cover can be found to insure their survival.

The strongly flowing stream of life in animals that continues generation after generation is likewise tremendously adaptable to the changing seasons. Deep snow and freezing temperatures will drive some species, like elk and deer, to migrate out of the high country. They drift down to lower levels and sheltered valley bottoms where browse is available to tide them over the tough winter weather. Others, like the mountain goats,

mountain sheep, and species of predators that prey upon them, simply shift to terrain where the raging winds clear the ridges and slopes of snow sufficiently for them to find roughage. On these southwest sides of the mountains, they manage to make it through the hard weather of the high country.

For other warm-blooded animals, the passing seasons are compelling enough to drive them underground. Seeking shelter in dens, burrows, tunnels, beneath upturned trees, or in rocky caves, they sleep away a good share of their lives in peaceful hibernation. The hoary marmot of the alpine meadows will sometimes spend as much as eight months out of the year in hibernation. Other species alternate their winter rest with brief interludes when they emerge to bask in a few hours of intense winter sunshine.

So it can be seen that the passing seasons do not spell out the same thing to all species. In a multitude of different ways each has discovered a unique manner in which to adapt itself to its mountain realm. An acute awareness of this soon settles down over anyone who comes to the mountains with a sensitive spirit.

To me, as a man who has spent years studying, photographing, and enjoying wildlife in the high country, the adaptation of wildlife to this magnificent realm is a never-

ending source of amazement, wonder, and joy. So many people, especially writers, scientists, and casual visitors have depicted the role of wildlife in the mountains as little else than a fierce battle for bare survival. I do not see it that way. True, the terrain and climate are tough. But so too are the species which have made it home and revel in it.

In fact there is a dimension of delight and keen exhilaration to mountain weather which is known only to those who spend time amongst the peaks.

Just a few weeks ago, a friend and I decided to go up into the alpine country close to our homes. It was late October, and the first great snow of the winter season had come in on a three-day storm. As we moved up through the timber, the snow grew steadily deeper. Trees were bowed and bent beneath their white burdens.

At first it seemed like an empty world of white. Apart from the occasional cry of a raven, not a sound disturbed the intense stillness. Even my companion and I felt constrained to speak in quiet whispers. Here, under the radiance of a blue sky and brilliant sunlight, our spirits were hushed in awe and wonder. A thousand points of sparkling light shot back from the glinting surface of the snow. And in every direction we could see newly mantled mountain ranges reflecting the radiance that shone from their slopes like a hundred diamond facets.

Suddenly I spotted the fresh tracks of a big mule deer in the snow. He had been moving strongly. His leaps and bounds had taken him across the rough ground with easy grace. The season of the early rut was upon him. He was responding to its impulse with dash and verve. He was a mountain monarch reveling in his upland realm.

We hiked on farther, gradually gaining altitude. As we broke out of the trees well above the last fringe of the forest, we came across several bands of California bighorns. This is a species of wild sheep native to the interior rangelands of British Columbia. Formerly their range extended through Washington, Oregon, and California. These bands before us were in magnificent condition, superb in strength and vigor.

With the greatest of ease, they dashed across the slopes draped in snow. The big rams were in hot pursuit of the ewes. This was their mating season, and the sheep displayed enormous energy and vitality as they moved effortlessly across their majestic mountain world.

Nowhere was there even a hint of apprehension or fear because of the blizzards that had just wrapped their upland world in deep folds of white. If anything, just the opposite was true. Here was a superb life form thriving amid a seasonal change which was an accepted part of their life pattern.

Once again there engulfed my very being the most profound and powerful sensation and awareness. *This is my Father's world.* It is beautiful in design. It is remarkable in its intricacy. It is superb in its harmony.

The mule deer, the raven, the mountain sheep, and even the mountain cottontail whose tracks soon crossed ours, were all a part of the profoundly inspiring panorama. Each were moving in rhythm with the changing seasons. They were components and attributes of a single setting, scene of magnificent grandeur that had been unfolding for uncounted centuries.

It was our great honor and privilege to be there briefly to witness this drama, to share momentarily, as mere men in this majestic mountain interlude.

My friend and I turned our tracks toward home. The brilliant sunshine glowing off the glinting surface of the snow had warmed our faces and lightly tanned our cheeks. Our eyes were bright, glittering, gay with the sheer delight of the long views and the gorgeous day. There was a spring to our steps and renewed vigor in our bodies. We had come and tasted and drunk deeply from the invigoration of this lofty landscape. Its peace and serenity had settled deep into our souls.

Moving softly through the trees, I turned to take a long, last, lingering look at the snow-mantled meadows. To my unbounded delight, I saw a handsome coyote standing on a rock outcrop that pierced the sykline. He was alert, scanning the slopes spread out below him. Like a statue cast in fresh, glistening bronze, his glossy winter coat shone gold in the sun.

He was in no hurry. He stood there in the snow in utter silence, unmoving, posing in full view, as though giving my memory time to have his portrait etched in it forever. And in truth it did leave an indelible imprint. It was a setting of such beauty that it remains undimmed, untarnished by the passing of time.

It was two men enriched in spirit who came down off that mountain that evening. Such experiences are beyond the bounds of our human capacity to measure. We have no scales or standards by which to measure, weigh, or define such delights. They are the essence of the eternal. Their delight, their joy, their uplift, their inspiration, their enrichment are beyond definition. They cannot be gauged by any material standards.

And so it is that in the presence of such pristine glory, some of us quietly bow our hearts. In utter sincerity and simplicity, we breathe, "Thank You, Father, for such beauty and such pleasure!"

But all of this is because of the changing seasons that swing gently across the earth.

In saying all this, there is no intention of minimizing the severity of mountain weather in winter. I have fought my way through too many storms to know better. I have been out in bitter blizzards with the temperatures plunging well below zero. I have faced winds with ice on their edges that clean took one's breath away and chilled to the marrow.

Yet when the storm had passed, the wind had abated, and the landscape lay hushed, it could again be exquisite. Again and again I have gone out to walk alone under winter moonlight. Its glow, accentuated by starlight shining on the snow slopes, creates a realm of such rare, fragile beauty that it resembles a fairyland of fantasy. The final touch is added when the lonesome cry of a coyote wavers across this winter wonderland. This is the wilderness in its most mellow mood.

But even in the highest mountains, winter does not last all year. As the spring sun climbs higher in the skies, increasing warmth spreads across the slopes. Ridges and

crags and cliffs, exposed to the sun, absorb its heat. Snow begins to melt. Water starts to trickle over the stone. The sound of tinkling drops is heard in the hills.

Around every forest tree and shrub, a small circle of snow sinks downward to the soil. Gradually its diameter increases. Finally a fragment of the earth appears beneath the trees. It is littered with the debris of leaves, twigs, cones, and bark shredded from the trees and stripped from the boughs by winter blasts.

On the exposed slopes and upland grassland, dark patches of soil and rock and sod appear. Quickly they pick up heat as the expanse of bare ground grows greater. Suddenly, almost as if by the wave of a magic hand, wild flowers and grasses thrust themselves up through the vanishing snow and chill-surfaced soil. Thousands of avalanche lilies and glacier lilies adorn the glades and meadows.

Soon they are followed by a host of other early flowering plants. They spread their glory across the slopes in commingled greenery and glowing colors. Spring comes suddenly, intensely, and with enormous vitality.

Spring in the mountains is a season not only of new color and pulsing life, but also of

/97

astonishing sights and sounds. There are the first faint cries of birds, some on wing high overhead, others moving in flocks through the trees, still others that have come to stay for the summer, now staking out their territorial preserves with stirring songs. Some of these are shy and retiring, others loud and bold. Everywhere bird calls echo and reecho across the valleys.

But above and beyond all this, there are the deep, somber sounds of splintering ice and moving waters. Every little stream and mountain rill begins to flow. They fill the cool, crisp air with the music of running water. The accumulated flooding inundates the river bottoms. The winter ice cracks, booming as it breaks into variegated blue and white blocks.

On the highest peaks, spring is a time of tremendous upheaval. Alternating temperature changes between warm days and chill nights produce repeated freezing and thawing. Gaunt slabs of rock are split off the crags. They thunder and roar over the cliffs, sending thousands of tons of stone, shale, and snow rumbling down the slopes. Huge cornices of snow, accumulations of ice, and deep drifts of packed winter snow avalanche into the valley bottoms. Trees are sheared off like brittle wood chips. Boulders, bushes, and trees are torn from the soil, swept away in the thundering maelstrom.

Amid all this sound and fury, if one treads very carefully and listens very acutely, one will hear other tiny notes. There will be the bleating of a newborn lamb or kid, the low call of an elk cow to her calf, or a doe to her fawn, the gentle rumble of contented bear cubs suckling their mothers, the splash of a beaver breaking water in his pond.

Summer is the season perhaps best known to most people who come to the high country. The snow and ice have withdrawn to linger only in the deep draws and north slopes seldom touched by sun. The trails and roads are open to those who wish to explore. The days are hot enough to be pleasant and the nights brief enough to be endured without hardship.

This is the time when the forests put on their new growth of greenery. The deciduous, broad-leaved trees spread themselves in new glory. The aspens and poplars shiver in every passing breeze, turning their thin-stemmed leaves like windmills in the wind. The conifers acquire a tender green as new needles replace the old, dark clusters. Their branches and limbs are adorned with ten billion brilliant, bursting buds of golden cones and blossoms. On close examination they rival the charm of any Christmas tree trimmed by human hands. They are much less gaudy, but much more in elegant good taste.

Under hot summer sun the trees perfume the air with their own, special fragrance. There is the pungency of pine and spruce and fir. Commingled with it is the delicate bouquet of Balm of Gilead, junipers, and alder shoots.

The meadows and forest glades are awash with a profusion of color from hordes of wild flowers. Every color known to man is found in these mountain meadows. Blues, reds, yellows, pinks, golds, browns, and greens come in a diversity of shades beyond description.

Amid all this light and color, animal and bird life appear to be scarce. The birds are busy nesting quietly and rearing their broods of young. The other wildlife are sheltering from the sun in the deep shade of the trees. There, too, they find respite from the insects which otherwise torment both them and men so mercilessly.

The return of the first frosts announce the advent of autumn in the high country. In northern regions these can come as early as August. Overnight an amazing change comes over the landscape. Color commences to flame in the foliage of plants, shrubs, and trees. The insect swarms are silenced. Clear blue skies follow nights of sharp, brittle frost. The whole world comes under a pensive mood.

Somehow one senses that the weeks which remain before the uplands are locked again in the grip of ice and snow are few and precious. Even if the season happens to be open and warm with the faint, blue haze of Indian summer, there are signs all around that this glorious season cannot long endure. So it must be relished. It must be enjoyed to the limit, while it lasts.

Everywhere foliage is ablaze with brilliant hues. From the most lowly wild strawberry plants to the patches of blueberries in the great burns, scarlet and crimson colors delight the eye. The dwarf willows, birches, and beeches glow gold and bronze. The aspens, poplars, and mountain larches are awash with tints of brilliant yellow. The maples and red osier dogwood are crimson red and deep purple. The forests and valleys pulse with light and color, signaling the end of the seasons.

The inspiration, delight, and uplift of such beauty always bring to mind the majestic lines from Psalms 121:1, 2

> I will lift up mine eyes unto the hills, from whence cometh my help.
> My help cometh from the Lord, which made heaven and earth.

Perhaps most exciting of all is the appearance of wildlife. With the advent of cool, crisp weather and its freedom from insects, deer and moose, elk and caribou graze in the green glades, no longer seeking shelter in the timber. Birds, small mammals, and other life forms feed happily on the ripened fruit, berries, cones, and seeds that have matured under summer sun.

All the high country is preparing for winter weather. And when the first heavy snows drape the peaks in shining white, the ultimate artistic touch has been added to a landscape alive with gorgeous colors.

And God said, "Let the waters bring forth swarms of living creatures, and let birds fly above the earth across the firmament of the heavens."

Genesis 1:20 RSV

6
Mountain Wings

There is a gigantic ebb and flow to the tide of insect and bird life that moves back and forth across the mountains. It is every bit as pronounced and powerful in performance as the massive migrations of bird life north and south across the continents.

Those people who, in growing numbers, are becoming enthusiastic nature lovers, find an exciting fascination in this phenomenon. There are said to be roughly fifty million outdoor bird watchers in North America today. This is more than twice the number of those who buy licenses to hunt birds or shoot game.

Many outdoor enthusiasts naturally and instinctively are drawn to high country. Not only does it offer them a great variety of terrain to explore, but it also provides beautiful vistas with a wide array of winged creatures, birds, butterflies, insects, and wind-borne seeds. All of these add enormous interest and diversity to their days on the mountain trails.

These fluctuating populations of winged forms are of course closely linked to the changing seasons, interwoven with them in a close-knit pattern of exquisite and intricate design.

For seven years I owned a very rustic log cabin high in the interior mountain country of British Columbia. It lay in a secluded valley above a beautiful lake cradled between rugged hills. One of the tremendous thrills of living in that gentle place was the ongoing pageantry of the wildlife around us. The fluctuating populations of birds, especially, that would come and go with the passing seasons were a never-ending source of pure joy. Within a radius of a mile of my door, I identified nearly one hundred different species.

In spring, even before the last of winter's snow had melted into the ground, the slopes of the hills would resound with a thousand bird calls. Some of these feathered visitors had flown several thousand miles from their southern wintering grounds in Mexico, Central America, and the southwestern United States.

I vividly recall sitting at the rough wooden table where I used to write, by the large open window, watching the great flocks of geese moving northward across the mountains. Their cries would fill the skies and come drifting down to a rough woodsman at work, writing in the cabin.

There was a wild, haunting, uplifting thrust to their calls. Unable to contain myself, I would rush to the door, dash outside, and shade my eyes from the sun to watch the majestic migrations against the burning skies. Several times I stood on a high outcrop not far behind the cabin. There, flocks of geese, flying very low, pushed past me with great, powerful strokes of their pinions. Their swift passage overhead, at nearly sixty miles an hour, produced a surging, pulsing rush of wind behind each wingbeat. It was a stirring sensation.

There were other great migrations that passed through my upland world. Sandhill cranes, whistling swans, myriads of ducks, as well as lesser birds, swept overhead, bent on reaching either northern nesting grounds or southern wintering ranges.

Sometimes at night, if one went out under the star-studded skies, the haunting, high-pitched cries of small birds passing through the night could be heard. They were

flying swiftly, under moon and stars, across the high country. Some were going from north to south. Others would be moving from east to west, from the prairies to the Pacific Coast, in search of either summer or winter ranges.

In all of these gigantic migrations there remains a marvelous mystery. It far transcends all the technology and scientific experiments conducted to discover how birds accomplish such magnificent feats of navigation. It is the wonder of a bird in flight. It is the marvel of fledglings finding their way unerringly across unfamiliar terrain with absolute surety. It is the incredible ability to fly surely through tempestuous storms and blinding blizzards, across high mountains, great valleys, and sweeping plains or deserts.

Often as I have stood, alone awestruck, my face upturned, my ears attuned to the distant call of the flocks in flight across the high country, my spirit has been stilled. This is no accidental happening. This is no mere interaction of physical and chemical stimuli. This is a drama of divine design. This is a poignant pageantry played out upon the planet under the direction of my Father's hand. This is His world, even if some parts of it have gone very much wrong through man's selfish mismanagement and misuse.

Yet every spring and every fall the magnificent migrations of the birds are dynamic reminders of the enduring grandeur and concern of my Creator. This passage of thousands of winged bodies in bold, brave flight reassures me again that our Lord meant what He said when He was amongst us, "Not a sparrow falls to the ground, but your Heavenly Father knows it, sees, and cares."

From time to time one of these "fallen ones" comes into my hands. Two years ago I found a gorgeous, golden, western meadowlark lying on the road. It had been killed in full flight by a speeding automobile. I stopped to pick up its still-warm body. The bird was beautiful in the glory of its breeding plumage. Tenderly it was wrapped in tissue and taken to a taxidermist friend. Today it graces our home, a beautiful part of the great outdoors.

But the mountains have much more than just the great bird migrations that pass through in spring and fall. They also are enlivened by exciting populations of bird life that spend all or part of the year here in residence.

Scattered throughout the forests, open burns, glades, and mountain meadows, as well as marshes, ponds, lakes, and streams, there is a dazzling array of birds. In fact there are hundreds of species that vary in size from the regal trumpeter swans to tiny hummingbirds not much larger than an oversized bumblebee. Some hummingbirds resemble winged jewels flashing in the sun as they whiz from flower to flower in erratic flight. Nor are they timid little things. I have watched their males fight furiously with dive-bombing tactics and flashing wings that resembled combat planes in action.

For me, as a mountain man, there are perhaps three aspects to bird life in the high country which have left the most poignant memories.

The first of these is the wondrous, stirring flight of the eagles and hawks. Somehow the sight of these great birds of prey has always given a touch of wild splendor to the mountains, not quite matched by anything else. I can spend hours watching the soaring flight of an eagle cutting circles in the clouds. Borne aloft on the rising updrafts of the mountain thermals, there is a majesty to their movements that quickens my pulse. They are an integral part of the high country that lifts a man's spirits and sets him to singing.

I shall never forget one morning in the Rockies. I came around a rock ridge suddenly to feel the fierce rush of a huge golden eagle sweep just over my head. He was scouting the mountainside for ground squirrels. He had not seen me coming behind the ridge. And

as his great wings, outstretched six feet, rushed past me, I sensed close at hand the overwhelming power and strength of his majesty.

A totally different aspect of bird life that I revel in is the shy, plaintive calls of various birds that one often hears but seldom sees. There are the whistled notes of song sparrows; the distant drumming of woodpeckers on dead trees; the low, muted thunder of grouse that echoes through the woods; the twilight songs of thrushes, warblers, and wrens; the haunting hoot of the great owls.

Even in the heavy timber of the forested valleys, these sounds lend life and interest to one's days. It takes patience and some perseverance to spot the songsters. It is much easier to see them in the forest glades or mountain meadows. Especially above timberline, their songs are wafted across the great basins in undulating, flutelike notes. The commingled sounds of tumbling streams, wind in the trees, and assorted bird songs are a mountain serenade not soon forgotten.

The third dimension of birdlife which has gripped my interest is the remarkable manner in which some fairly large birds survive in the mountains as permanent residents. These are the various species of grouse, the ptarmigans, the ravens, and some owls.

Each of these in its own individual way has become very well adapted to the harsh conditions of winter in the high country. It takes a very tough and hardy bird to endure the fierce winds, low temperatures, deep snow, and long nights of mountain winters. Especially so when the feed available is sparse. The ability to survive on a diet of pungent tree buds or a few scraps of flesh that can be found amid a white, chill, and forbidding wilderness commands my deepest respect.

Whenever I come across these species and see them bravely reproducing year after year amid such challenging surroundings, I am deeply impressed. For even the harsh, raucous call of a raven winging over his wilderness, is the resonant cry of one who has met his challenge in triumph.

For a great many birds, however, the mountains would be a hostile and forbidding realm were it not for the prolific array of plant and insect life upon which they feed. It is the spectacular and swift appearance of these lower life forms that provides a banquet for the birds. Tender new shoots of grass, bursting buds, swarms of insects, the wide array of seeds, berries, and wild fruits of all sorts provide the birds with their foundation food supplies.

Even for the larger birds of prey there emerges from dens, burrows, and rock piles a prolific variety of small mammals. Picas, ground squirrels, chipmunks, mice, marmots, squirrels, and voles of a dozen sorts are all links in the complex food chain that enables the great, winged hunters to flourish. They must compete with coyotes, bobcats, mink, marten, and even bears for this foundational source of sustenance. All are interwoven in

the intricate ongoing life of the high country. The balance and counterbalance of all these interrelated factors are fascinating to observe.

For the visitor who comes to walk softly, to sit quietly, to listen long, and watch with interest, the mountains are an amphitheater of never-ending enchantment. He moves in a region of remarkable diversity. Here nature expresses itself in a thousand different forms. Often the lavish display is set against backdrops of soaring peaks, wide, wild valleys, untamed rivers, great brooding marshes, and shadowed forests.

Each type of terrain is a complete world of wonder in itself. The interplay of its component parts is not something accidental or a matter of happenstance. Again and again I have marveled at the manner in which some rare species of bird, animal, tree or plant has established itself in the precise niche or habitat best suited to it. Perhaps the seeds have been borne for uncounted miles on the mountain winds. Mayhap others have traveled across the country by birds in flight or animals in migration.

Always, ever, there is the eternal push of plants and animals, insects and birds into new territory. This is all a part of the exciting order and design so apparent in the wilderness world. The powerful forces in the biota, planned and programmed by our Father, are proceeding with meticulous precision. The pageantry of seeing one species supplant or succeed another in amazing progression elicits our profound admiration.

None of this was planned or processed by the mind of man. At best, if he is humble in heart and receptive in spirit, he can only observe and understand a little of the complex interaction of the biota. Even those of us who have spent most of our years in the outdoors recognize how little we understand. Yet this does not diminish our delight in every new adventure that is brought to us by the high country.

This past autumn, a friend and I decided to hike up a rugged canyon. There was a wild stream that tumbled between its steep walls of multicolored stone. Uncounted centuries of snow-fed waters rushing and rumbling down its bed had worn away the hard rock, until in places it was polished smooth as marble. Here and there young trees and hardy

shrubs had struck root in the crevices of its broken walls. Their green and golden foliage hung over the swift water in delicate sprays. It was a superb setting.

We paused to unwrap our lunches. Sitting beside the singing stream, I was startled to see a handsome weasel working his way down the boulder-strewn bed toward us. He was totally unafraid. Erratically, he darted in and out of the broken rocks and tangled brush piles. Suddenly he began to dash up and down a high, vertical bank that towered some forty feet up the canyon wall behind us. He could race up or down this formidable, steep face with utter impunity. He would suddenly stop in mid-dash, clinging to the vertical surface like a fly on a wall. It was an amazing display, lasting a full half hour in broad daylight.

Never before had I been in such prolonged contact with one of these formidable little hunters. I marveled that no passing hawk or eagle had seen him. In an instant he would

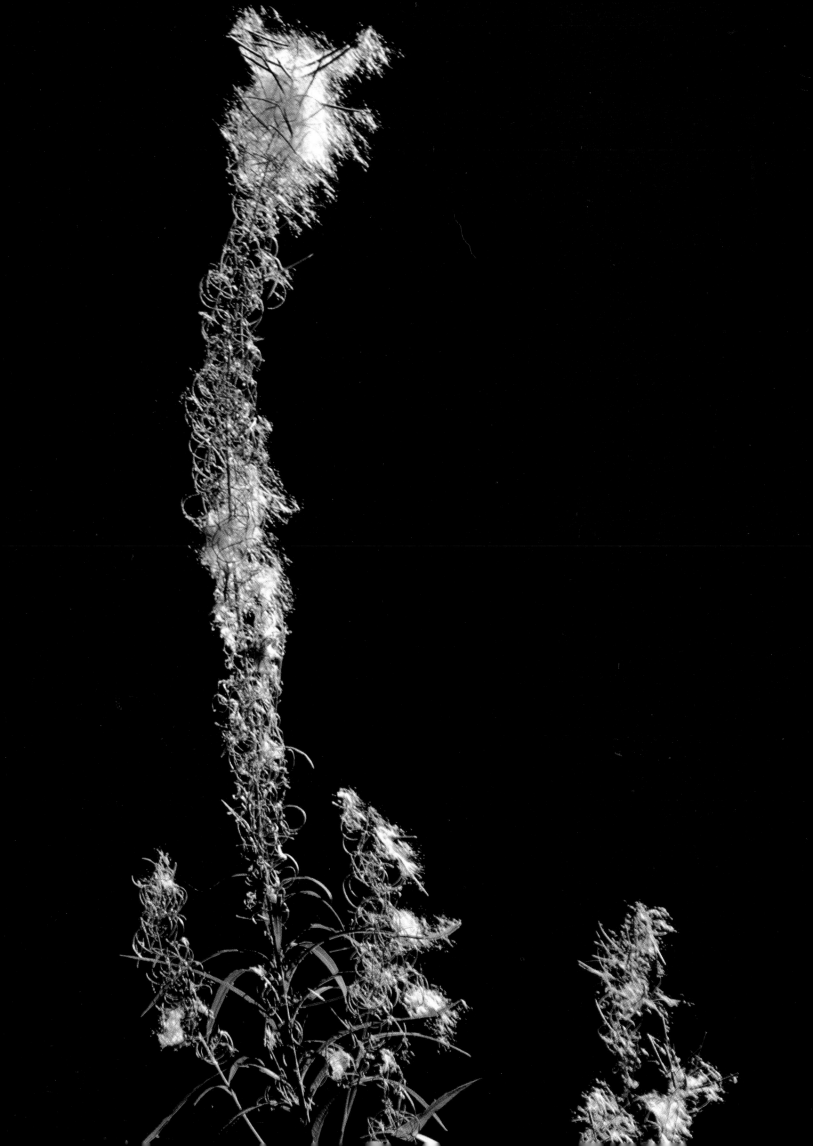

have been plucked from his vulnerable position. It was a momentary bit of mountain drama, difficult to explain yet tremendously fascinating.

Behind this interlude, there were impulses and drives at work that had been in motion from the dawn of time. And in this we two men rejoiced. Tramping home quietly under the trees, we knew we were richer for the unforgettable day.

God said, too, Let the land yield all dif-
ferent kinds of living things, cattle and
creeping things and wild beasts of every
sort; and so it was done.

Genesis 1:24 KNOX

7
Mountain Wildlife

Mountain country, in general, the world over, is rich with wildlife. Yet there is something of a paradox in this for many people. For, though they may visit the mountains
again and again, they may seldom see any wild animals of significance, apart from a few
birds. The exceptions are the national parks and wildlife sanctuaries, where wildlife
becomes accustomed to human beings. It is there that travelers or tourists will encounter
animals in fairly close proximity along the roads and trails.

Even then most people lament the scarcity of wild animals. It has been pointed out
earlier in this book that the seasons have much to do with wildlife movements. In winter
they evacuate the higher, exposed terrain, swept and buffeted by blizzards. They migrate down into the more heavily timbered areas where there is shelter from the storms
and forage to feed on in the forests. Others go into hibernation.

Similarly, in the heat of late spring and summer, when insects torment all wildlife, they will seek relief from the mosquitoes, flies, and gnats in the cool, deep
shade of the trees.

This means there are only a few weeks in spring and fall when the likelihood of seeing
wildlife in significant numbers is very real. Of course, for the person familiar with their
behavior and acquainted with their life habits, the wild ones can always be found.

Very often, a visitor may have hiked for miles and seen perhaps nothing more than an
occasional squirrel or chipmunk. Yet, unknown to him, he may have been quietly
observed by a score of eyes belonging to wild creatures who were lurking quietly in
seclusion as he went past.

119

There is a tremendous challenge in all of this. The ability to find and stalk wild animals in their native habitat has long been part of the great thrill to hunting. And in more recent times the increasingly popular pastime of wildlife photography has produced its own adherents.

With the advent of accurate telescopic sights for firearms, the need to stalk game to close quarters was more or less eliminated. Similarly, in wildlife photography the introduction of long lenses, with their remarkable magnification, has meant that even amateur outdoorsmen can obtain beautiful pictures of animals.

It may intrigue the reader, if he or she is at all interested in wildlife photography, to know that the longest lens used to obtain any photograph in this book was a 135 mm, Hektor lens. Used on my sturdy and reliable III F Leica camera, it is a remarkable lens of enormous resolution that has accompanied me on my mountain rambles for the past twenty-five years.

It may very well be asked why I have not resorted to longer lenses. There are three main reasons. First of all, I was born and raised in Kenya. It was, during my boyhood, still very much a frontier country in Africa. All of us youths were familiar with firearms. From my earliest years I handled rifles and shotguns. They were a very important part of life. The man skilled in their use could be sure of meat for the table and a degree of protection from predators. Wildlife was prolific. It surrounded us on every side.

Because of this, from my earliest years I learned to hunt skillfully and stalk stealthily. A great part of the supreme satisfaction in the pursuit of game was to pit one's own skill and bushcraft against that of the quarry. So when in later life I turned to photographing wild animals, I still wished to preserve in my work this element of suspense and challenge that comes from a careful stalk and close approach to animals in their own habitat.

The second reason for not using longer lenses is a bit more obscure. In fact it may even seem rather absurd. But for me, as a mountain man, a great part of the pure joy and thrill of my mountain days has lain in close, intimate encounters with wildlife. Those who may have read some of my earlier books will know that to encounter animals at close range, to study them in their native surroundings, undisturbed by my presence, was one of the main purposes for being there. It was worth all the tough trails, long climbs, and heavy packs that I carried into the high country.

What was more, I was among the first of the wildlife photographers to discover that wild animals were not always as fierce, dangerous, or vindictive as they had been depicted. I learned early in my career as a field naturalist and outdoor photographer that there was a tremendous thrill in just quietly spending time with wildlife. It was possible to establish rapport even with shy species. And as one moved amongst these wild friends of hoof, wing, or paw, a remarkable sense of respect and comradeship developed. Out of this there emerged an enormous compassion and concern for the conservation of both the creatures themselves and their wondrous upland world.

Not all of these intimate interludes with the wild ones produced prize photographs. As often as not I might return from the mountains with only a handful of outstanding pictures. But one thing was always certain, I came back a richer man, my memory enlivened by exciting experiences that no one could ever take from me. Something of the agony and ecstasy of those times has been recounted in detail in some of my books, such as, *Africa's Wild Glory*, *Canada's Wild Glory*, *Under Wilderness Skies*, *Under Desert Skies*, and *Travels of the Tortoise*.

So it can be seen that a deliberate refusal to use long lenses actually compelled me to spend time establishing close contact with wild animals. In all of this there has been a dimension of profound joy and deep pleasure. I have been close enough to Olympic elk, bighorn rams, grizzly bears, Rocky Mountain goats, and even coyotes to talk to them, call to them, and share a few days of their mountain world with them. And these were wild ones in sometimes very remote, wilderness terrain.

The third very good reason for not using powerful, long lenses was the very simple one of sheer weight. When I went to the high country, it was with a backpack. Whatever I needed, be it my sleeping bag, food for the trip, extra clothing, or camera gear, it had to be hoisted onto my own shoulders. Most of my life I simply could not afford to hire horses, guides, aircraft, or any other modern mode of transporting people into tough terrain. What I went in with was carried by the strength and stamina of my own sturdy legs and stout heart.

The net result was that my camera equipment was of the barest minimum and lightest weight. What was more, I knew that by using nothing longer than a 135 mm lens, it could be hand held steadily without the added support of a tripod or other impedimenta which would hamper my movements in the high country.

Because of all this, my expeditions were not cluttered up with a multiplicity of gadgetry. Nor was I cumbered with the complexities of caring for a lot of expensive equipment. I traveled lightly. I could move with a maximum of freedom. My mind was

free to give maximum attention to my mountain world. My spirit was set to singing as I wandered across the high country in happy comradeship with the wildlife which was such a wondrous part of this wilderness.

Out of these exciting years in the high country, a profound and powerful philosophy of life took form. There came upon me the enormous awareness that all living creatures—man included—share this sphere as fellow travelers through time and space. Each of us has the supreme and sublime right to relish his brief interlude on the planet.

To none of us, not even man himself, is given the mandate to impoverish or exploit another for selfish purposes. In fact it came to me most clearly that it was to human beings that the lofty responsibilities of husbanding and conserving the native resources and pristine glory of our environment were entrusted. These were not ours to abuse, misuse, squander, or waste. God, our Father, had set us as integrated individuals amid a most remarkable array of life forms. Each of us had an essential part to play in contributing to the well-being of the other. We were and are all interdependent, interwoven in the intricate and incredibly beautiful web of life.

Not every reader will by any means understand what I mean by this. But perhaps I can explain just a little. Let us take a grizzly bear for example. It may very well be asked what in the world does this big, powerful creature have to contribute to the ongoing of our

/123

twentieth-century world? How can it be said that he is really entitled to survive and thrive on a planet pulsing with some three billion human beings?

The replies to these questions, from our human standpoint, will be given at greater length in the last chapter. Suffice it to say here that the grizzly has made a remarkable impact on human history. The part this great bear played, in the past, as a powerful predator is interlaced with the frontier folklore of our own people and the tribal traditions of the North American Indians. The strength and majesty and presence of the great, long-clawed bear stood for dignity, courage, and command in all our early culture. Songs were written and tales told depicting the might and vigor of these great bears. And to this day, those of us who have spent time studying them in the high country of their wilderness world are immeasurably impressed by their enormous vitality, fantastic strength, and noble grandeur.

The grizzly, despite his retiring habits and demand for great spaces in which to thrive, deserves to survive. He is a magnificent and noble expression of his wild realm. He is not an anachronism. He is an emblem of that untamed, free spirit of the wilderness so essential for man's own well-being.

The strength and stamina of the grizzly has been reproduced in various art forms all through the centuries. Both in the Indians' culture and our own, this monarch of the mountains has been portrayed as a symbol of superb majesty, whether carved in a totem pole or painted on canvas.

This awe and respect for a specific life form comes home poignantly to any person who has spent time in close proximity and association with it. Up until the middle of the twentieth century, our general ignorance of wildlife behavior was appalling. The very

superficial knowledge which did exist was condensed in large part from the pursuit of wild animals by hunters, trappers, and sportsmen.

One of the truly remarkable phenomena of the entire conservation movement in the last forty years is the intense interest shown in wildlife. Both men and women all over the world, from the arctic to the tropics have given their time and strength and minds and means to live with wild animals in prolonged and intimate association. Out of this, there has emerged an enormous fund of incredible information showing the remarkable behavior of wildlife in their native habitats.

The net result has been the generation of a mighty ground swell of public concern for the preservation of wild creatures in wild places. Beautiful books, fantastic films, prodigious reports, and painstaking research by thousands of dedicated investigators have aroused our people to the plight of endangered species.

And this is to be commended.

It is as it should be.

What many forget is that in its early inception some of the leading figures fighting in the forefront of this cause were individuals with a genuine Christian concern for the preservation of wild places and wildlife in general. The names of men like John Muir, Theodore Roosevelt, Jack Miner, and others stand out boldly in the ranks of those who were fearless in their fight for their wild friends.

Admittedly it has taken us a very long time indeed, as a race, to be brought to the place where we recognize in wildlife something of more value than just meat for our stomachs or skins for our backs or sport for our outdoorsmen. As a matter of fact, it has taken us thousands of years.

In my recent book *Rabboni . . . Which Is to Say, Master,* the point is made that in the initial environment prepared by God for human habitation, it was intended that man should be a preserver and not a plunderer of the earth. Here I quote from the chapter entitled "And Then, Men."

To be true to Himself, Christ had no alternative but to be the supreme conservationist. What He had brought into being He was concerned should be preserved. And the initial picture of man painted for us in Scripture is that of one placed in a magnificent environment with definite instructions to tend and husband it with care.

The Lord God placed the man in the Garden of Eden as its gardener, to tend and care for it.

Genesis 2:15 LB

Contrary to much distorted teaching on the subject, early man had no need to subdue nature. He found himself a harmonious part of the whole scheme of creation. That he was endowed with an intellect superior to that of other life forms in no way implied it was for the purpose of subjecting them to his personal whims. The sense in which he was given "dominion" over all the earth implied, rather, a profound responsibility for the preservation and perpetuation of his earth, with all its beautiful life forms.

This is an enormously important point. It completely escapes most scholars and theologians. Yet it is inherently true to the very person and nature of Christ. The very essence of His character is *to care*. And by this I mean to care

pawfuls of snow. The cub protested loudly and vehemently. Yet she ignored his cries. She rolled and tumbled him gleefully, rubbing him vigorously with the snow until his coat shone bright in the spring sunshine.

This ablution completed, she led him down onto a patch of heather nestled between some stunted spruce trees. There, before my wondering eyes, she laid down, turned over on her back, and invited her cub to drink deeply from her distended breasts. This he did eagerly and contentedly, at peace with all around.

I had been a silent, unknown witness to a scene of enormous tenderness, care, and

consummate pleasure. And it had moved me profoundly.

It was a midwinter's day: sharp, bright, brittle with a fierce frost freezing the air. The thermometer reading stood at thirty-five degrees below zero. Bundled up in wool cap, scarf, warm mitts, heavy bush jacket, and my high-lined boots, I had been on the trail for several hours. The exertion of plowing through the mountain snow kept me warm. But I was also charged with the excitement of my surroundings. I had broken out of heavy timber and stumbled on an open expanse of water in a mountain marsh.

A mistlike wraith of humid air hovered over the scene where warm spring water bubbled into the pond. It was a very large pond, impounded by a curving dam of mud and sticks now covered in a soft mantle of snow.

In the pond was a newly mudded beaver lodge. It was obviously occupied, so I decided to shelter in some trees nearby to see if there would be any signs of life. To my surprise a small, dark, slate gray bird flew out over the water and landed on the ice edge. It was a water ouzel. With carefree abandon, he suddenly plunged into the dark water and dived beneath the surface. In a few moments he was back up on the ice, swallowing an insect larva he had retrieved from the bottom of the pond.

His repeated diving aroused a young beaver from his lethargy in the lodge. For he, too, soon surfaced quietly to see what had disturbed his domain.

Satisfied that all was well, he decided to cut a few limbs from the poplars he had wedged in the mud for his winter food supply. It was a scene seldom enacted in broad daylight. But there I sat unnoticed, relishing a bit of drama as ancient and remarkable as the splendor of the mountains that encircled this little stretch of open water in midwinter.

It was autumn in all of its still and misty splendor. The days were warm, blue, and bright under a friendly Indian summer sun. The faint haze of fall hung in the valleys like the last lingering smoke from a distant forest fire. A light sprinkling of sugar-icing snow dappled the gaunt, gray granite of the mountain tops. All the river bottoms and stream sides pulsed with golden shafts of brilliant poplars that provided a perfect foil to the dark green forest foliage.

The nights were cold, chill, and crackling with frost. It spread its icy fingers across every still pond and marsh. The reeds and sedges were bronzed and browned by the early touch of winter. Frost flowers formed on the thin ice, and a white carpet graced every open, grassy glade.

Through the still, chill mountain air, every sound was amplified and carried clearly across the countryside. The far-off warning howl of a wolf hunting, the staccato yelps of a coyote calling to its mate, the shrill bugling of bull elk challenging each other to battle, all electrified the atmosphere and captured my attention.

I wandered down a lonely streambed, drawn by the rattling of antlers and thrashing of heavy bodies in the trees. Two bull elk were locked in fierce and furious combat. Heads down, flanks heaving, legs lunging, they struggled in the heat of the rut to overcome. All along the open verges of the riverbank, they battled.

This was the ancient rite of conquest. It was the victor who would claim the cows. It was his offspring who, next spring, would move quietly with their dams to the high country. This was the fierce battle for the survival of the fittest.

Suddenly, with a tremendous lunge, one bull forced the other over the bank. The loser dashed into the river, seeking escape in its swift flow. The battle had been brutal. The destiny of the herd was decided.

I could go on recounting scores and scores of little interludes like these. But those tales have been told elsewhere. These few are to give the reader a momentary glimpse into the wonder of our Father's world, hoping they will be an inducement for you to go out and relish its joys for yourself.

And God said, Let us make man in our image, after our likeness: and let them have dominion over the fish of the sea, and over the fowl of the air, and over the cattle, and over all the earth. . . .

Genesis 1:26

8

Mountain Men

In the opening pages of this book it was pointed out that my forefathers were the fierce mountain men of the Swiss Alps. They were, and still are, a hardy breed who cherish and husband their high country with remarkable affection, loyalty, and wisdom. The strength and stability of this tiny, landlocked nation has become all the more remarkable in an era of international upheaval and disintegration.

In large part this is because of the painstaking care the Swiss people have shown in preserving the resources of their upland realm. They have taken very tough steps to insure that the natural assets of their mountain world will be conserved for generations yet to come. In this they have set a pattern that more profligate people would do well to emulate.

In many mountain regions there is a growing, accelerating, frightening tendency to exploit the high country with terrible greed and callous indifference. For those of us who love this upland country, the carnage wrenches a cry of protest from our innermost beings. Our mountains were never meant to be raped and ruined. It is intended rather that they should be cherished and esteemed. They must be preserved from those who would plunder them for selfish gain.

All too often, certain, special sectors of our society see in the mountains a ready opportunity to extract great wealth for themselves. Yet the overall loss to all the rest of us may well be enormous.

The logger, sawmill operator, or paper mill owner looks on the forest as so many board feet of lumber or tons of pulp to be marketed at the highest possible price. In the past many of our most magnificent stands of timber were felled with incredible waste. Steep

ridges were logged off, then left to the ravages of rain and weather that wreaked awful erosion on the slopes. Logging roads and skid trails were abandoned with impunity. Slash burning that left the landscape destitute and denuded was done; the land was even burned black to bedrock in some regions.

Fortunately, in recent times some of these trends have been turned around and even terminated. Steps have been taken to conserve and manage forests with enlightened care and long-range management in view. Improved harvesting techniques, proper reforestation, the seeding of roads and trails, more efficient use of slash and waste are beginning to demonstrate that modern men take their mandate of forest management seriously and conscientiously.

Very much the same sort of enlightened trends are apparent in the grazing of upland ranges by sheepherders and cattle men. There was a time when the magnificent mountain meadows of the West, especially, were regarded as free range for anyone audacious enough to claim and seize it.

Fierce rivalries raged between stockmen. Many of these hardy pioneers were not the least bit concerned about the horrendous damage done to the uplands by their hordes of "hooved locusts." Overgrazing and terrible ruination of the high open ranges were carried on with utter impunity. Entire species of fine native grasses were literally eaten out of existence, to be replaced by poverty grass, weeds, and noxious plants unfit even for wildlife to use.

Some of the most beautiful alplands were denuded. Extensive erosion, great gaping gullies, and loss of soil were a part of the pathetic game played out on many public lands.

Meadows were marred. The fragile plant communities were fractured. And wildlife was hard pressed for winter range.

But much of this is being altered. Scientific range management, precise population control of grazing pressures, reseeding, and even improved fencing are now being used in many mountain regions in a concerted endeavor to restore the mountain meadows.

All of this is heartening and helpful. It gives hope for the future. It bears witness to the fact that modern man realizes that in his dominion over the earth he must, in fact, exercise mature and intelligent responsibility.

The same sort of principles are also being applied in the whole realm of mining and mineral exploration. Not only is this true of the mining industry itself, but also of the entire oil and gas community.

At their best, these human enterprises are only relatively short-lived. Few are the mines that have life expectancies exceeding a few, short years. Their extractive process is such that once a deposit of coal, copper, cobalt, uranium, gold, silver, or other ore is exhausted, they have no choice but to pull out and move elsewhere. Precisely the same is true of oil and gas fields.

But during the brief period of their operation, enormous damage can be and often is done to the mountain terrain. Great open pits, tailing dumps, mine shafts, cut lines, and a maze of roads frequently mar the countryside where these activities are carried on.

Happily, an aroused public awareness of this damage has resulted in very rigid controls in some regions. The man with a mineral lease is no longer a freewheeling operator who can make his mint then move out. Now steps must be taken to restore the ground to some semblance of its former condition. Topsoil must be replaced. Reseeding and replanting of ravaged areas must be done. And for all of this we should be grateful.

A community consciousness is even beginning to gain ground in such difficult and thorny enterprises as power plants, ski runs, hunting regulations, and sport fishing. The old frontier philosophy that the wilderness was up for grabs, that it fell into the fist of anyone fierce enough and fast enough to seize it, is dying rapidly.

There are simply too many people coming around to the view that the mountains and their resources were not just made for man's exploitation. There is a rapidly growing segment of society which sees more in streams and rivers than just so many kilowatts of electricity or tons of salmon to sell. They see on the flowered hillsides more than so many prime yearlings or tourist dollars from ski runs and lodges. They see in wildlife more than so many hunting licenses or guide fees or sales of sporting goods.

Power companies can no longer plug any canyon with a dam to turn their turbines. They cannot kill and still the wild, white waters that inspire and stir the spirits of so many wild river enthusiasts. Nor can ski lodge developers or hunting lodge entrepreneurs brazenly build their gaudy edifices wherever their own particular interests dictate. Those days are gone. And today they must comply with the will and wishes of multitudes of mountain enthusiasts who prefer to have some of their wild world untouched, untarnished by the coarse hand of modern commercialism.

For some of us, in truth for increasing multitudes of us, it is infinitely more important to breathe the clean, fresh wind from a pristine wilderness than luxuriate in the comfort and luxury of heated lodges and lighted streets. Something deep within us demands the challenge of untamed heights and great, untouched valleys. To survive amid the stifling stultification of our times, we need the healing of places wild, free, and open.

Even in our great national parks, now so beloved, yet trampled half to death by mounting hordes of visitors, new and sterner controls are coming in. A person cannot just pitch his tent or light his fire wherever fancy dictates. Nor are the back-country trails open to anyone who slips a pair of hiking boots on his feet or a pack on his back.

The days are pretty well done when a mountain man or woman could just head over the next hill to see what lay beyond the blue horizon. Now his or her movements are

pretty well bounded and defined by regulations, permits, and passes. The wilderness can tolerate only so much pressure from people. Too many tramping feet, too many scattered campfires, too many hatchets in inexperienced hands, too much noise and commotion can readily reduce a realm of quiet beauty to just another tourist trap.

The gaunt, beautiful Sierras where John Muir moved amid so much solitary grandeur are now invaded by millions of visitors every summer. He came to the high country in humble spirit, aware at every turn in the trail that this was indeed his Father's world. Where he walked in quiet, profound meditation, now ten thousand others follow in his footsteps. Theirs can be the same exhilaration, the same uplift, the same inspiration, provided this pristine realm is not polluted or despoiled by the passing crowd.

In wisdom and with ever-increasing foresight, those responsible for the preservation of our mountains realize that travel here must be restricted. No longer can we afford to punch new roads into every valley or along every ridge we see. We cannot allow all-terrain vehicles or high-powered motorcycles to roar wherever their drivers may wish to go. We must restrict four-wheel-drive trucks, snow toboggans, power boats, and even aircraft. With the aid of such modern devices, a handful of intruders can easily desecrate the entire wild domain.

All of the complex legislation and restrictive regulations now coming forward to control the movement and activity of man in the mountains are a blessing in disguise. To those of us who have known and relished the high country in its heyday of freedom, these rules may seem tiresome and even a bit threatening. But they are for the benefit of all.

Not only is this the way to insure that people who love and enjoy the mountains will not be disappointed, but also it is really the only way in which their wildlife and natural beauty can be preserved.

There is no simple, single solution to the host of prickly problems posed in nature conservation. To the end of time there will have to be ongoing adjustments made to accommodate men to the mountains. This is inevitable simply because of burgeoning human populations and the proliferation of twentieth-century technology. Increasingly, the two combined exert mounting pressures on the planet.

Yet, in the face of all this, it is appropriate to assert that we who are Christians should be in the forefront of those who care for the high country. We can see it as a superb segment of our Father's world. It is worthy of our strength and effort. It is here many of us can find moments of magnificent inspiration. It is here we can walk quietly to find refreshment of soul and rejuvenation of body. And because the mountains bear this ability to restore us in wholeness, they are worthy of our love.

It is out of this realm that has come much that is the finest and most noble in our literature, art, music, and scientific thought. The mountains are a majestic repository of inspiration for our people. They deserve our deepest respect and widest acclaim. They are an integral part of our Father's design for both the enjoyment and responsibility of us, His earthly children. Let us be grateful He gave them to us to love and to cherish.

There may not be given to each of us the opportunities to know, love, and speak for

wild places that were given to John Muir. But still we can be loyal in our defense of even those small, serene spots which have become precious to us personally—those places where some of the serenity and tranquility which is our Father's intention should enrich our lives can be found.

Few, if any of us, will ever be placed in positions of great national prominence, as was President Theodore Roosevelt when he was instrumental in establishing the great National Parks System. Yet this does not preclude us from energetic and enlightened participation in those societies dedicated to the preservation of natural beauty and native splendor.

It is most unlikely that any of us will ever live in some choice location, as Jack Miner did, where he could band thousands of wild, migratory birds and provide a sanctuary for them on his own private land. But we can, with quiet joy, relish those inter-

ludes, when, alone in some secluded spot, we give humble thanks for the glory of our Father's handiwork.

For just a few minutes one day, amid the duties of a busy schedule, I slipped down to a nearby mountain lake and sat amongst the great, gray rocks. A dark storm had just passed. The wind from the hills swirled across the sandy shore. There was a break of blue sky opening to the south.

Almost before I knew it, a small flock of curlews alighted at the water's edge near me. They began to probe for feed along the shore. It was an engaging bit of natural drama. There was a sense of the ageless ongoing of the biota around me.

As I sat there, I was surrounded, as men have been from the dawn of time, with the pageantry of the planet; there swept over me again the calm assurance that God, my Father, cares not only for the curlews which had flown thousands of miles to alight on

this tiny stretch of sand, but in His love, He also cares for me.

There came afresh to my spirit those magnificent lines from the Scriptures:

> Now Christ is the visible expression of the invisible God. He was born before creation began, for it was through him that everything was made, whether heavenly or earthly, seen or unseen. Through him, and for him, also, were created power and dominion, ownership and authority. In fact, things were created through, and for, him. He is both the first principle and the upholding principle of the whole scheme of creation.
>
> Colossians 1:15–17 PHILLIPS

In this awareness lay great repose!

154/

Photographic Notes

The slides chosen to illustrate this book were drawn from several thousand of outdoor subjects taken during the last thirty-five years.

Most of them were taken with a Model III F Leica camera, using either a 50 mm, 90 mm or 135 mm lens.

Apart from about half a dozen, all of them are either on Kodachrome, Kodachrome II, or Kodachrome 25 film.

Mountain Light

Mountain Waters

Mountain Land Forms

Mountain Meadows and Forests

Mountain Seasons

Mountain Wings

Mountain Wildlife

Mountain Men